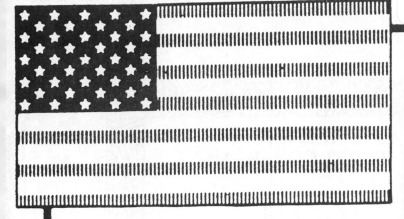

HE'S WATCHING YOU

EVIL AGENDA OF THE SECRET GOVERNMENT

Exposing Project Paper Clip and the Underground UFO Bases of Hitler's Elite Scientific Corps
by *Tim Swartz*

Global Communications

EVIL AGENDA OF THE SECRET GOVERNMENT

ISBN: 1-892062-00-3

Editorial Director:
Timothy Green Beckley
Assistant to Publisher:
Carol Ann Rodriguez
Cover Art: Wes Crum

Free Catalog of Conspiracy Books From:
Global Communications, Box 753,
New Brunswick, NJ 08903

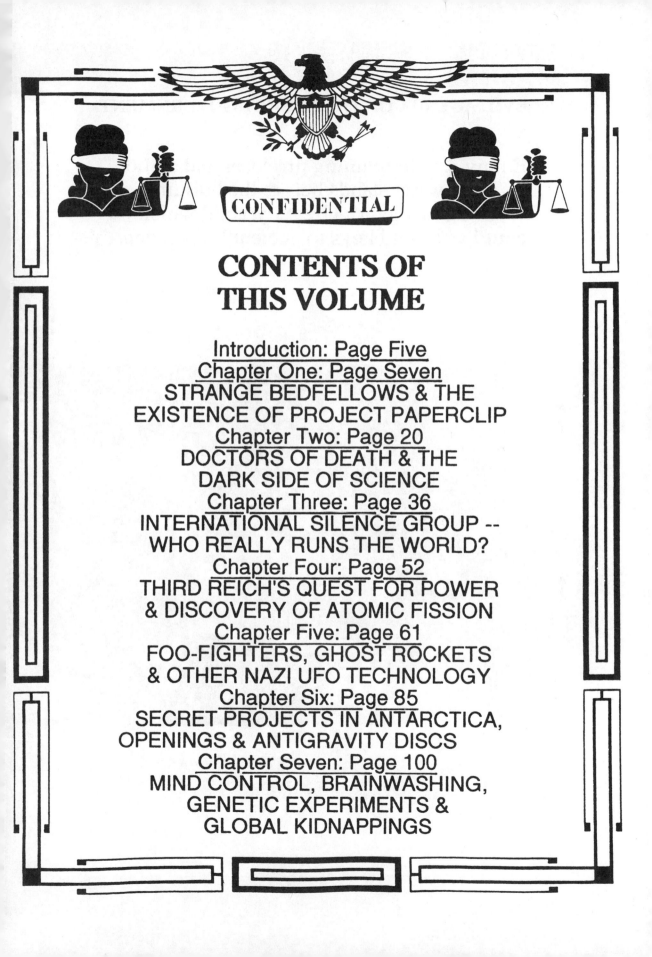

CONFIDENTIAL

CONTENTS OF THIS VOLUME

EVIL AGENDA OF THE SECRET GOVERNMENT

Emmy Award winning producer and author
Tim Swartz stands before the building
blocks of Egypt's Great Pyramid which
could well hold keys to ancient knowledge.

EVIL AGENDA OF THE SECRET GOVERNMENT

INTRODUCTION

Many people have a certain fascination concerning the Third Reich before, during and after World War II. This fascination may be because of the amazing ability that Hitler and his evil minions had in redeveloping post WW I Germany into a country that almost took over the world. Others are convinced that Germany and the Nazis were literally evil incarnate.

Despite the fact that Germany and the Nazis were considered "public enemy number one," many countries, including the United States, made deals with the former heads of the Nazi government. These deals enabled many Nazi officials, scientists and intelligence experts to avoid war crime charges, and live out the remainder of their lives in freedom and prosperity.

Some interesting evidence has been uncovered over the years that many high level Nazi officials were able to gain top level positions in the government and military of certain countries, including the United States. These so-called "former" Nazis may be responsible for certain conspiracies and other tragic events that have plagued the planet in the years after World War II. In fact, some people believe that the Nazis were not defeated, but simply went "underground" in order to re-group. Their plan for world dominance could still be underway, but this time, instead of being backed by one country, now they have the resources of many.

This book is an attempt to chronicle facts about the Nazis that have been kept hidden from the public for many years. How many people could accept the truth that nuclear war with the former Soviet Union was almost started by a former Nazi intelligence agent employed by the United States? How many could believe that UFOs might have been developed by Germany at the end of WW II? Who dares to acknowledge that the Nazis could still be around, biding their time, waiting for the perfect moment to once again strike terror in the hearts of an unsuspecting population.

EVIL AGENDA OF THE SECRET GOVERNMENT

Various Earth made disk are known to exist, some of which date back to World War II and German science.

Chapter One

STRANGE BEDFELLOWS AND THE EXISTENCE OF PROJECT PAPERCLIP

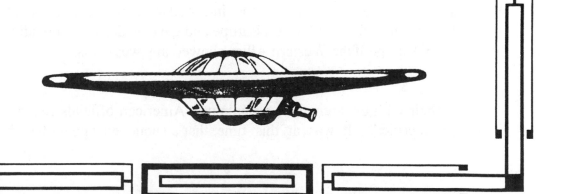

EVIL AGENDA OF THE SECRET GOVERNMENT

In 1945 the greatest war which the world has yet seen was over. It was a war whose ramifications reached to the ends of the earth and affected practically all of its inhabitants. Since that time the story of World War II has become shrouded in a mist of legends and disinformation. Top secret material discovered by researchers over the years has revealed that commonly held beliefs about the war and its players are erroneous, and possibly fraudulent. The second world war still has an influence on the world today. To ignore its story runs the risk that it may all happen again.

The fear that a reunified Germany could threaten the world in the future has not gone unnoticed in the shadowy world of conspiracy theorists. Some people believe that the Third Reich did not die at the end of the war, that it survived by disappearing into the background, waiting for the right moment to resurface and begin anew. Others say that Hitler and his disciples escaped into the night, to a secret city hidden in Antarctica. What is known is that Hitler's dreams did not disappear with the allies' takeover of Berlin. In one way or another the Nazis have lived on and perhaps flourished in secret, aided by the very powers that at one time considered the Third Reich to be the enemy.

OPERATION PAPERCLIP

By the end of the war the ever-growing conflict between the United States and the Soviet Union was causing great concern in Washington. The huge American military force that had played an important role in the defeat of Nazi Germany had been demobilized and only a small U.S. military establishment remained in Germany. Washington had believed that Russia, too, intended to demobilize. Instead, Stalin had enlarged his military force in Eastern Europe and gave evidence of intending to move into Western Europe if the Western Allies showed any weakness.

With their military strength at a minimum, American officials realized that the situation was critical. It was at this time that a subtle change in the official U.S.

attitude toward the Nazis took place. It was decided that the Nazis who had been active on the eastern front and were knowledgeable about the Soviets and their tactics could be of help. This would also include certain German and Austrian scientists and engineers. When the Soviets seized Czechoslovakia and established the Berlin blockade, the Pentagon decided to ignore the public outcry against the Nazis and instead form a secret alliance between the United States and the Third Reich against the common enemy of Communism. This U.S. secret project was called Overcast in 1945, and later changed to Operation Paperclip in March 1946. The British equivalent program was code-named Backfire.

REINHARD GEHLEN

Probably the most influential Nazi to work for the United States was named Gehlen. "Reinhard Gehlen," writes author Christopher Simpson, "Hitler's most senior military intelligence officer on the eastern front, had begun planning his surrender to the United States at least as early as the fall of 1944." Of the several hundred high-ranking Nazi officers who switched sides at the end of World War II, Gehlen proved to be the most important of them all.

In early March 1945 Gehlen and a small group of his most senior officers carefully microfilmed the vast holdings on the USSR in the military intelligence section of the German army's general staff. They packed the film in watertight steel drums and secretly buried it in remote mountain meadows scattered through the Austrian Alps.

On May 22, 1945, Gehlen and his top aides surrendered to an American Counter-intelligence Corps (the CIC). Gehlen immediately asked for an interview with the commanding officer and offered the United States "his intelligence staff, spy apparatus, and the priceless files for future service. Gehlen was sent to Washington and his offer was taken.

EVIL AGENDA OF THE SECRET GOVERNMENT

When The War Department's Joint Intelligence Objectives Agency formed to investigate the backgrounds and form dossiers on the Nazis, Gehlen met with the CIA director Allen Dulles. Dulles and Gehlen hit it off immediately. Dulles promised Gehlen that his Intelligence unit was safe in the CIA. As promised, Allen Dulles delivered the Nazi Intelligence unit to the CIA, which later opened umbrella projects stemming from previous Nazi research (MK-ULTRA/ARTICHOKE, OPERATION MIDNIGHT CLIMAX). The CIA-Gehlen agreement in practice guaranteed the continuation of the all-important Abwehr division of the German General Staff.

Hundreds of German army and SS officers were quietly released from internment camps and joined Gehlen's headquarters in the Spessart Mountains in central Germany. When the staff had grown to three thousand men, Gehlen opened a closely guarded twenty-five-acre compound near Pullach, south of Munich, operating under the innocent name of the South German Industrial Development Organization.

Within a few years the Gehlen apparatus had grown by leaps and bounds. In the early fifties it was estimated that the organization employed up to 4,000 intelligence specialists in Germany, mainly former army and SS officers, and that more than 4,000 V-men (undercover agents) were active throughout the Soviet-bloc countries. Gehlen's spy network stretched from Korea to Cairo, from Siberia to Santiago de Chile. When the Federal Republic of West Germany became a sovereign state in 1955, Reinhard Gehlen was openly recognized as the official intelligence arm of the Bonn government.

How important was the Gehlen Organization, as it became known, to the history of the Cold War? Christopher Simpson's research documents that it was perhaps the most significant element of all: " The Org became the most important eyes and ears for U.S. intelligence inside the closed societies of the Soviet bloc." "In 1946 U.S. intelligence files on the Soviet Union were virtually empty." Says Harry Rositzke, the CIA's former chief of espionage inside the Soviet Union. Rositzke worked closely with Gehlen during the formative years of the CIA and credits Gehlen's organization with playing a "primary role" in filling the empty file folders during that period.

EVIL AGENDA OF THE SECRET GOVERNMENT

Reinhard Gehlen in full Nazi parade uniform
at height of Germany's march through Europe.

EVIL AGENDA OF THE SECRET GOVERNMENT

"Gehlen had to make his money by creating a threat that we were afraid of." Says Victor Marchetti, formerly the CIA's chief analyst of Soviet strategic war plans and capabilities. "So we would give him more money to tell us about it. In my opinion, the Gehlen Organization provided nothing worthwhile for the understanding or estimating Soviet military or political capabilities in Eastern Europe or anywhere else. Employing Gehlen was a waste of time, money, and effort, except that maybe he had some counter- intelligence value, because practically everybody in his organization was sucking off both tits."

THE GAMES SPY'S PLAY

By "sucking off both tits" Marchetti is referring to the fact that Gehlen's elaborate operation was penetrated by Soviet spies at the very time it was our most important source of intelligence upon which the Cold War was based. For sometime many Americans had worried that Gehlen's group had been infiltrated by Soviet agents and this concern increased as the CIA worked more and more closely with the Germans.

One such critic was Arthur G. Trudeau, who had headed the 1st Constabulary Brigade in Germany during the Berlin blockade and airlift. In 1953, although he was stationed in the Far East, he warned Washington during his visits to the capital that with Gehlen becoming privy to CIA secrets and slated to know NATO confidential plans in the future, his organization should be checked closely for Soviet infiltrators. However, Trudeau was ignored and two years later, after he repeatedly made his warning while chief of army intelligence, he was relieved from this post and sent back to the Far East.

Ignoring Trudeau was a serious error. The fact was that the Communists had infiltrated Nazi intelligence long before Gehlen switched sides. One such agent was Victor Schneider, a former SS officer in the section commanded by Heinrich Muller, who had helped investigate and destroy the "Red Orchestra" Soviet spy network in

EVIL AGENDA OF THE SECRET GOVERNMENT

Germany during WWII. Late in the war, however, he ended up in the Sachsenhausen concentration camp for ignoring Muller's orders.

After the war, the KGB leaders forgave him for his part in the destruction of the "Red Orchestra" when they concluded that he could help them in his position as a bookkeeper in Konrad Adenauer's Christian Democratic Party. The Soviets by this time were convinced that Adenauer would lead the new West German government when it was formally established, and they wanted contacts within his organization. Unfortunately for the western powers, Gehlen had also hired Schneider to work for his own organization and had recommended him to Adenaurer. Moreover, through Gehlen's influence, Schneider's wife Erika had obtained a position in the Ministry of Defense. The two were sending dozens of copies of important documents to East Germany every week.

Possibly the one man who did the most damage to Gehlen's group was Heinz Felfe, chief of counterespionage at Pullach. Despite the fact that Felfe was responsible for the denouncement of the Schneiders, he was unable to uncover the source of additional leaks to the Soviets. These leaks enabled the Soviets and East Germans to round up hundreds of Gehlen's agents. The reason for Felfe's inability to discover the secret culprits is obvious, since Heinz Felfe, Gehlen's trusted associate was the double agent everyone was seeking.

It is amazing that Felfe could have remained in his position so long without detection. It wasn't until 1961 that he was arrested. During the intervening ten years Felfe worked his way up to a key position at Pullach with help from the Russians. In 1958 he was appointed to the Soviet desk in Gehlen's counterespionage section. This was an ideal position for Felfe. He was able to copy documents at will and forward them to the KGB's East German headquarters at Karlhorst. He photographed the names and background information of West German agents, warned Soviet officials when it appeared certain that Soviet agents were going to be arrested, sent the Russians copies of all interrogations of their people who had defected to the West, and undermined

EVIL AGENDA OF THE SECRET GOVERNMENT

Gehlen in every possible manner. Yet he did it with such flair and cunning that Gehlen never suspected him.

The defection of an East German SSD officer to the West in 1961 was Felfe's downfall. The defector insisted that there was a Soviet agent in the highest rankings of Gehlen's organization. On October 27, 1961, a radio message from the KGB to Felfe was intercepted. Gehlen admitted that Felfe had completely outwitted him and ordered his arrest. It was the beginning of the downfall of Reinhard Gehlen and had a serious effect on NATO secrecy for several years after Felfe's arrest.

Gehlen's influence on the Cold War however cannot be overemphasized. By deliberately exaggerating Soviet intentions and capabilities in order to alarm the United States, the Gehlen organization increased cold-war tensions and manipulated them to Germany's advantage.

Perhaps the most important effect of the Gehlen organization was to introduce "rollback" or "liberation theory" into American strategic thinking. Rollback was a political warfare and covert operation strategy which had its genesis in the Third Reich Ostministerium headed by Alfred Rosenberg. This strategy entailed enlisting the aid of dissident Soviet ethnic minorities to overthrow the Soviet Union. In return, these minorities and their respective republics were to be granted nominal independence while serving as satellite states of "Greater Germany."

In its American incarnation, liberation theory called for "rolling back" communism out of Eastern Europe and the break-up of the Soviet Union into its constituent ethnic Republics. Lip-service was given to initiating democracy in the "liberated" countries. Liberation theory was projected into mainstream American political consciousness through the Crusade for Freedom. This enormous CIA domestic media campaign not only established liberation theory as a dominant element in American strategic thinking but also projected European fascists associated with the Gehlen milieu into positions

14

of prominence within the powerful ethnic voting blocks in America. The Gehlen imports combined with domestic reactionary elements to form a powerful fascistic and ultimately triumphant political engine.

In his book on America's recruitment of the Nazis, *Blowback*, Christopher Simpson notes that Gehlen's alarmist reports helped heighten tensions between the United States and the Soviet Union during the Cold War. "Gehlen provided U.S. Army intelligence and later the CIA with many of the dire reports that were used to justify increased U.S. military budgets and intensified U.S./USSR hostilities."

Even though the Russians were still trying to recover from the devastation caused by the war, Gehlen's exaggerated reports about an imminent Soviet attack, came close to touching off a new war several times. "The CIA loved Gehlen because he fed us what we wanted to hear," former CIA officer Victor Marchetti told Simpson. "We used his stuff constantly, and we fed it to everybody else: the Pentagon, the White House, the newspapers. They loved it. But it was hyped up Russian boogeyman junk, and it did a lot of damage to this country."

In 1948 Gehlen nearly convinced the United States that the Soviets were about to launch an assault on the West. He advised that the West should strike first. Fortunately, they didn't. Later, during the 1950's, his erroneous claims that the Soviets had outpaced America in the military buildup fueled fears about the so-called missile gap. Classified Army and CIA documents from that time reveal that former Nazi intelligence agents had slowly infiltrated the American military, government and large corporations to their highest levels. While the United States scrutinized everything the Soviets were doing, little did they realize that a more sinister influence was secretly working among them.

John Loftus, who was the federal prosecutor in the Office of Special Investigations of the Criminal Division of the Department of Justice wrote in his book, *The Balarus Secret*, "In a way, we Americans are the last victims of the Holocaust, imprisoned by the secrets of the Cold War, locked in the fortress of lies. In a democratic society, there is only one hard way to liberation: Wahrheit macht frei, i.e., Truth produces freedom." The truth is that Washington used fascists against the Soviets as it has done clandestinely since the Bolshevik Revolution and since the unsuccessful U.S. invasion of Russia during the Civil War that followed. In turn however, the Third Reich found a safe haven in the United States to continue their master plan of world dominance.

Of those Nazis who were recruited to work for the United States, Operation Paperclip brought 118 German scientists to work on missile research. These scientists included Wernher von Braun and Arthur Rudolph, both of whom had directed research on V-2 rockets in Germany. In Operation Crossbow and Overcast, another 494 Nazi scientists and engineers were brought into the U.S. to work in weapons development and research.

The War Department's Joint Intelligence Objectives Agency (JIOA) conducted background investigations of the scientists. In February 1947, JIOA Director, Bosquet Wev, submitted the first set of the scientists' dossiers to the State and Justice Departments for review. Samauel Klaus, the State Departments representative on the JIOA board, claimed that all the scientists in this first batch were "ardent Nazis." Their visa requests were denied.

Wev was outraged. He wrote a memo warning that "the best interests of the United States have been subjugated to the efforts expended in beating a dead Nazi horse." He also declared that the return of these scientists to Germany, where they could be exploited by America's enemies, presented a "far greater security threat to this country than any former Nazi affiliations which they may have had or even any Nazi sympathies that they may still have."

One such scientist was Arthur Rudolph, who joined the Nazi Party in 1931. Rudolph was Director of the Mittelwerk subterranean rocket factory, also called

EVIL AGENDA OF THE SECRET GOVERNMENT

"Dante's Inferno," from 1943 to 1945 where 52,000 prisoners turned out 6,000 V-2 rockets. Rudolph's prisoners were used as slave labor, forced to work 72 hours a week and fed only 1,100 calories a day. They were beaten when they fell behind schedule. Twenty to thirty thousand died from lung and heart disease because of poor ventilation. Prisoners worked in knee deep water in the tunnels. In the summer temperatures were well over 100 degrees and freezing cold in the winter. Those too sick to work were sent to their death in the crematoriums at Auschwitz or hung from beams on underground cranes. Rudolph was responsible for these mass executions.

From 1951 to 1961 Arthur Rudolph was employed by MARTIN MARIETTA, in charge of research and development of the Pershing missile. In 1954 he became a U.S. citizen. He also headed the Saturn project for NASA and received the highest civilian honor, the Distinguished Service Award. In 1984 he renounced his U.S. citizenship and returned to Germany. Of the estimated 10,000 Nazis that found a haven in the U.S. only a handful ever left the country.

The Pentagon prevented the Immigration Department from conducting investigations of their Nazis. Military Intelligence "cleansed" the files of Nazi references. By 1955, more than 760 German scientists had been granted citizenship in the U.S. and given prominent positions in the American scientific community. Many had been longtime members of the Nazi party and the Gestapo, had conducted experiments on humans at concentration camps, and had committed other war crimes.

In a 1985 expose in the *Bulletin of the Atomic Scientists*, Linda Hunt wrote that she had examined more than 130 reports on Operation Paperclip subjects, and every one "had been changed to eliminate the security threat classification." President Truman, who had ordered no dedicated Nazis to be admitted under Operation Paperclip, was evidently never aware that his directive had been violated. State Department archives and the memoirs of officials from that era confirm this. In fact, according to Clare Lasby's book *Operation Paperclip*, project officials "covered their designs with such secrecy that it bedeviled their own President; at Potsdam he denied their activities and undoubtedly enhanced Russian suspicion and distrust," quite possibly fueling the Cold War even further.

Another good example of how these dossiers were changed is the case of Wernher von Braun. A September 18, 1947, report on the German rocket scientist stated, "Subject is regarded as a potential security threat by the Military Governor." The following February, a new security evaluation of Von Braun said, "No derogatory information is available on the subject. It is the opinion of the Military Governor that he may not constitute a security threat to the United States."

Why were so many Nazis welcomed into the United States, while many of those they persecuted were virtually excluded? The main reason was that the Nazis were also fervent anticommunists, and because Communism was a threat to the capitalist social order. Meanwhile many of these mass murderers continue to live in comfort using false identities provided by the U.S. government and forever shielded from prosecution. Still, others have continued their activities in Latin America and Europe under CIA direction.

Operation Paperclip was halted in 1957, when West Germany protested to the U.S. that these efforts had stripped it of "scientific skills." Paperclip may have ended in 1957, but for the CIA and the defense department, this was just the beginning. A secret laboratory was established and funded by CIA director, Allen Dulles in Montreal, Canada at McGill University in the Allen Memorial Institute headed by psychiatrist Dr. Ewen Cameron. When it was at its height in drug experiments, operation MK-ULTRA was formed. This was the brainchild of Richard Helms who later came to be a CIA director. It was designed to defeat the "enemy" in its brain-washing techniques. MK-ULTRA had another arm involved in Chemical and Biological Warfare (CBW) known as MK-DELTA. The "doctors" who participated in these experiments used some of the same techniques as the Nazi "doctors." What is ironic about Dr. Cameron is that he served as a member of the Nuremberg tribunal who heard the cases against the Nazi doctors.

EVIL AGENDA OF THE SECRET GOVERNMENT

Most historians would have you believe that just about every escape
Nazi had been captured and had been put on trial no later than
the Nuremberg Trials. As it turns out this was NOT at all the case. Many
"favorable" Germans were allowed to come to America where they
assisted early CIA members in developing advanced aerial technologies.

CONFIDENTIAL

Chapter Two

THE DOCTORS OF DEATH AND THE DARK SIDE OF SCIENCE

EVIL AGENDA OF THE SECRET GOVERNMENT

In order to further their political goals, the Nazis implemented programs of scientific inquiry to better understand and exploit the human species. These experiments, using so-called "social undesirables," stretched the limits of madness in their unfeeling torture of innocent victims. No one knows how many men, women and children died in the clutches of Nazi "mad doctors" who justified their fiendish experiments as for the good of mother Germany.

The important thing to keep in mind while studying this topic is that Nazi science experiments did not start in Germany. This type of human experimentation was world wide in its scope; the only distinction between Germany and other countries is that the former country took action to implement its pseudo-scientific dogma.

Doctors have always been thought of as the saviors of mankind, the healers, and caretakers of our utter existence. Even ancient civilizations revered the medicine men as having special power to protect life. The trust of a physician is sacred. This is why the practice of human scientific experiments by the doctors and scientists of the Third Reich is outrageous and shocking. The Nazi doctors violated the trust placed in them by humanity. The most painful truth is for the most part the doctors escaped their crimes against Humanity and lived a life, unlike their victims.

DOCTOR JOSEF MENGELE

Probably the best known of the infamous Nazi Doctors was Dr. Josef Mengele. Mengele was born March 16, 1911 in Gunzberg, Germany to Karl and Walburga Mengele. In 1935 Mengele was awarded a PhD from the University of Munich. On January 1, 1937, he became a research assistant at the Third Reich Institute for Heredity, Biology, and racial Purity, located at the University of Frankfurt. There he worked with Professor Otmar Freiherr von Vershuer, who would later get Mengele appointed at Auschwitz.

EVIL AGENDA OF THE SECRET GOVERNMENT

In May of the same year, Mengele joined the Nazi party (member #5574974). The next year, he became a part of the SS, got his medical degree from the University of Frankfurt and began training with the Wehrmacht. In 1939 he was wed to Irene Schoenbein and the next year he joined the Waffen SS medical corps. In 1940, he was appointed Untersturmfuhrer. In 1941, he went to the Ukraine with the Waffen SS and earned the Iron Cross. Became a war hero, earning another Iron Cross, the Black Badge for the Wounded, and the Medal for the Care of the German People. He was wounded and sent to the office of Race and Resettlement in 1942.

Dr. Mengele was known among both survivors and colleagues for his "flamboyant detachment." But the most famous image of Mengele has to be this doctor standing on the ramps coming from the trains. He would place his hands on his pistol belt and simply yell "left"(meaning that the individual was to be gassed) or "right"(meaning that the individual was to be sent to work).

Dr. Mengele's most famous research was that conducted on twins. Many describe Mengele's research on twins as almost passionate. This is, arguably, the reason he came to Auschwitz in the first place. Dr. Mengele became so prominent in the camp, that he was assigned three additional offices, besides the main SS doctor's office. He had one space in the women's camp, one in the men's and one in the gypsy's. Most of the time, the letters ZW were incorporated into twins tattoos.

One indication of his passion was in the fact that most twins, especially children, were allowed to keep their own clothes and their hair. Identical twins, however, were Mengele's favorites. There are hundreds of reports of identical twins being made to sit together for hours, nude, as Mengele examined them, comparatively. He left no bodily section untouched. One such story reveals two identical twins who, after being made to be together for so long, insisted on being interviewed together and whose voices were completely indistinguishable on audio tape.

EVIL AGENDA OF THE SECRET GOVERNMENT

Mengele was almost fanatical about drawing blood from twins, mostly identical twins. He is reported to have bled some to death this way. But Mengle's research could not be completed without the final step, dissecting twins. One famous account, tells of Mengele's assistant rounding up 14 pairs of Gypsy twins during the night. Mengele placed them on his polished marble dissection table and put them to sleep. he then proceeded to inject chloroform into their hearts, killing them instantaneously. Mengele then began dissecting and meticulously noting each and every piece of the twins' bodies.

Mengele was also interested in dwarves and physical abnormalities in general. It is widely believed that this extreme interest was due to Mengele's association of Jews as abnormal. Many say that he saw Jews as freaks. Mengele's quarters at Auschwitz included all manners of dwarves, giants, hunchbacks and other abnormal individuals.

Mengele's interest also turned to the usually rare disease, noma. This disease caused, basically, gangrene of the face and mouth. Due to the conditions at Auschwitz, this disease was extremely prevalent among Gypsy children. Mengele strongly believed that there was a biological and/or racial source of this disease, not that it was merely a bacterial infection. Mengele was known to kill for almost anything, as long as it was to have some tie to science.

Mengele's extensive research into eye color is particularly interesting. Many prisoner doctors report having routinely taken boxes filled with jars of eyes to and from Mengele's offices on a regular basis. Mengele was most interested in a condition of the eye, specifically the iris, called heterochemia. When this phenomenon occurs, a person has two different colored eyes. Mengele was most especially interested when he found heterochemic subjects that were twins.

As in most of the Nazi doctor's research, the results were to be used to further the Aryan nation. Mengele's eye color tests were no different. The research was merely a precursor to what would come next. Mengele soon began trying to actually change his victims eye color to blue, therefore "converting" them from their native race to the Aryan race. Mengele began injecting methylene blue into the subject's eyes. These victims were mostly children. In the scope of all Nazi doctor experimentation, this set of tests seemed unusually cruel. Most subject's eyes became extremely inflamed, but, in time, returned to their previous state. There is an account of at least one child dying from these injections and many others who went blind. Mengele's experiments had no basis in scientific fact. Almost each and every other Nazi doctor experiment was based on some type of scientific principle or hypothesis. Yet, it seems that Mengele took an extreme disregard for science, putting cruelty in it's place.

Even with all of his experimentation and infamy, the most interesting piece of Dr. Josef Mengele's life may be his post war days. Less than one year after his son Rolf was born (March 11, 1944), Mengele fled Auschwitz(January 1945). He turned up at the Gross-Rosen work camp and left well before it was liberated on February 11, 1945.

He was then seen at Mauthausen and shortly after he was captured as a POW and held near Munich. Then, remarkably, he came across papers from another doctor, Dr. Fritz Ulmann. Since Mengele had not had his blood type tattooed under his arm, as was popular at the time, he used these papers to slip by the Americans. They did not realize he was SS until it was too late.

Mengele then began to travel all over the world, using aliases such as: Fritz Ulmann, Fritz Hollmann, Helmut Gregor, G. Helmuth, Jose Mengele, Ludwig Gregor, and Wolfgang Gerhard. In 1949, Mengele went to Argentina. Five years later, his father visited him there, and in the same year, he divorced Irene Mengele. In 1958, Mengele married his brother Karl's widow, Martha. On June 7, 1959 West Germany issued it's first arrest warrant for him. That same year, he moved to Paraguay. Five years later, the University of Frankfurt, and that of Munich, disavowed his medical degrees.

EVIL AGENDA OF THE SECRET GOVERNMENT

Dr. Mengele's death has been somewhat of an enigma until recently. He was rumored to have died on February 7, 1949, suffering a stroke while swimming in Embu, Brazil. After the February 1985 trial at Yad Vashem, the body in the grave marked "Wolfgang Gerhard" was exhumed. In recent years, forensic evidence has assured that the body is indeed that of Dr. Josef Mengele.

DOCTOR HORST SCHUMANN

Dr. Horst Schumann is often referred to as an "old Nazi doctor." He joined the party in 1930. Many of his colleagues and associates joined 3-5 years after he did. Schumann was a major player in the prewar euthanasia program. He was the head of the mental facility of Grafneck. He had already begun to research in the field of surgical and X-ray castration.

Dr. Schumann came to Auschwitz on August 28, 1941. By this time, Himmler and Brack were already discussing plans for a major castration and sterilization project. Himmler envisioned a site at which a patient would walk in, and a technician would merely flip a switch, and a few minutes later, they would be sterile. He envisioned this site being able to sterilize between 3,000 and 4,000 people per day.

To raise the rate and effectiveness of X-ray sterilization, Himmler chose Schumann to do research. By late 1942, Schumann was busy at work in Birkenau's Block 30. Dr. Schumann usually chose young men and women in their late teens and early twenties. In Block 30 at Birkenau, female subjects were placed, naked, between two plates that pressed against both abdomen and back. The men had to place their genitals on a specially deigned plate. The subjects were then exposed to radiation for, as one doctor stated, "five to eight minutes." After the treatment, most women had their ovaries removed.

EVIL AGENDA OF THE SECRET GOVERNMENT

As with most Nazi surgical procedure, no attention was paid to health risks. The procedure used (a horizontal cut about the pubic area) was much more prone to infection than the alternate operation (abdominal opening). The ovaries were packaged and sent to an outside laboratory for testing. These procedures were often performed by another Nazi doctor, Dering. Dering also caused many women to bleed to death internally by not placing a small piece of the abdominal membrane lining on the end of the fallopian tube from which the ovary had been cut.

The male subjects did not fare any better than the females. Many survivors report that they had testicles (one or two) removed in a crude fashion. Many also allude to a small instrument, designed by Schumann himself, which, when inserted through the rectum, scratched the prostate and forced the man to ejaculate. All of this work was recorded and submitted to Himmler. It is estimated that about 200 men underwent both X-ray sterilization and castration. 90 of these operations took place on December 16, 1942. Almost 1,000 prisoners underwent X-ray sterilization.

As the war neared it's end, Schumann, too ran away. He fled to Ravensbruck, with Clauberg. Although he was discovered at the Nuremberg trials to be a criminal, he lived in Germany under a false name. After being identified there, he fled again, to Sudan, and became the head of a hospital there.

In Africa, Schumann seemed to have a change of heart. It seems he spent every waking moment treating Africans and studying sleeping sickness. However, after almost seven years, he was again identified. He then fled to Ghana. In Ghana, he was finally apprehended and given to West German authorities. By this time, he was weak from malaria and other diseases. Despite protests from Nazi hunters and the Israeli government, Dr. Horst Schumann was released without having stood trial, although he was recognized as a criminal at Nuremberg. Schumann died in Frankfurt, Germany in 1983.

EVIL AGENDA OF THE SECRET GOVERNMENT

DOCTOR RASCHER

Little is known about Dr. Rascher's Pre-War activities. However, by the nature of the power given to him, especially in his high altitude experiments at Dachau, it is apparent that he was a prominent member of the Nazi party in the pre-war years. Like the other doctors, Rascher was a member of the Nazi Doctors coalition, a group who eventually became the only doctors in Germany, as non-Nazi doctors were "removed" from their positions.

Dr. Rascher is probably most known for his experimentation at Dachau, concerning human resistance at high altitudes. He also conducted research in the fields of body temperature, membrane inflammation, and had some ties to the operation of the gas chambers. In addition to these experiments, Rascher also conducted tests on priests, and worked with incoming transports. Dr. Rascher conducted many different types of experiments during his tenure at Dachau.

Dr. Rascher's high altitude experiments were directly ordered by the heads of the Nazi party. Unlike some of the other experiments, this research was not conducted based on personal interest. Reichsfuehrer - SS Himmler called for these experiments, and Rascher was approved for the experiment by leaders of the Reich. The results were to be used to judge the effects of high altitudes on Luftwaffe pilots.

Rascher used a sealed chamber to conduct these experiments. He would then lower pressure and oxygen levels, to simulate rise in altitude. All subjects died. Rascher also had some subjects inhale pure oxygen preceding the experiment, to discover whether or not this would increase sustainable altitude. As most doctors did, Rascher reported his findings to the Reichsfuehrer. He also conducted detailed autopsies in which he discovered that large amounts of air (oxygen) were in the patient's blood arteries and veins at the time of death.

EVIL AGENDA OF THE SECRET GOVERNMENT

Dr. Rascher's body temperature experiments were, like his altitude experiments, conducted to gain results to be used by the Luftwaffe. The experiments, called for by the authorities in the party, were to simulate the effects on Luftwaffe pilots who were forced to parachute from their planes into the seas. Rascher used a variety of combinations in his experiments.

Subjects were dressed in either winter or summer Luftwaffe uniform. Next, they were placed in tubs of water with temperatures ranging from 2.5-12 degrees centigrade. Some subjects were placed under narcosis while others were not. The final choice in these experiments was either to submerge the brainstem of the subject or to leave it above water.

Rascher reported to his superiors on the results. He reported that among those patients whose brainstem's were submerged in water, all died. Though not as prominent as the cooling experiments, attempts were also made to test resuscitation methods on freezing subjects. Again, Rascher reported to his superiors, namely Brandt, on these issues and tests. The "warming tests" were much less successful than the cooling tests, as most subjects died.

Dr. Rascher conducted a small series of experiments that still stand in the shadows of his cooling and high altitude tests. Rascher had a special hatred of the church, as did most of the Nazi party. For these experiments, Rascher chose a group of 20 healthy priests from the camp. He conducted a series of tests concerning a cure for the purulent inflammation of certain membranes. In German, this was called phlegmone. Rascher injected the disease into all twenty priests. As a result, 12 priests died and the other 8 suffered severe skin burns and inflammations, as well as other diseases.

In addition to his experimentation, Dr. Rascher also had a hand in the transports coming into Dachau. Rascher also had a hand in developing the gas chamber into it's final form. It appears that Rascher was one of the men who first began experimenting with different types of poisonous gasses, ultimately helping the Nazis to arrive at the deadly Zyklon-B which they used from then on to eliminate their undesirables.

In one of the more obscure events at Dachau, Rascher was reported to have inspected those subjects who would not survive medical experimentation. It is reported that he would grab them by the thighs, and if he said "good", it meant that after death, the subject was to have his skin stripped from his body.

Ironically, Rascher was executed by the Nazi party following the war. It appears as though he and his wife were intermarried. This was strictly forbidden by the Nuremberg Laws of 1935. So, although Rascher was not present at the Nuremberg trials, many of his personal documents were used, as was testimony concerning him.

DOCTOR KARL CLAUBERG

Dr. Karl Clauberg joined the Nazi party in 1933. He quickly became a Gruppenfuhrer(lieutenant general). He also received the Nazi Golden Badge, given to party members for outstanding service. Before beginning work at Auschwitz in 1942, Clauberg was a noted professor at the University of Kiel. In 1937, at age 39, Clauberg received his Habilitation (an endowment that gave him lecturer and professorial abilities, based on extensive research in a scientific field).

Dr. Clauberg's work in gynecology, and specifically in pregnancy, led him to become an Auschwitz doctor in 1942. There he continued his studies in this area. His main objective was to develop a serum by which women could be sterilized by injection. Again, Himmler was behind the entire project. Himmler was the one who first precipitated the idea of creating an agent to produce blocking in the fallopian tubes instead of one which got rid of blockage.

EVIL AGENDA OF THE SECRET GOVERNMENT

With Himmler's help, Clauberg began his experimentation on animals, discovering that only a 5%-10% solution of Formalin would inflame the fallopian tubes to the point of blockage. This was to have been used by the Nazi party to make sure that none of the untermenschen (sub-human races) were allowed to breed.

His basic procedure included injecting the women with a colored liquid to check for prior fallopian blockage. When it was determined that there was no blockage, he injected another substance into the cervix. Based on documents and testimonies, this substance is believed to have been Formalin and/or Novocain.

At the largest capacity, Clauberg had more than 300 women in his famous Block 10. He encouraged them to stay by telling them that he would not only keep them from being sent to Birkenau(which meant imminent death), but also by telling them that he wanted to take them to his clinic in Konigshutte, very near Auschwitz. Clauberg's experiments, in Himmler's eyes, were so vital to the Nazi Biomedical Vision, that Himmler kept a file himself on this sterilization by injection.

On a personal level, Dr. Clauberg was a man who most found detestable. Many survivors speak of his crude, joking manner and of his general dislike by other camp authorities. One minor doctor interviewed after the war calls Clauberg "short, bald and unlikable." Dr Wirths, the head doctor at the camp is quoted as saying that, in the end, Clauberg had, "gone to the dogs, become an alcoholic, and a totally unscrupulous character." Wirth's brother, another doctor in the camp, described Clauberg as, "one of the worst characters I have ever met."

Towards the end of the war, Russian troops began advancing towards Konigshutte, where Clauberg had his clinic. He had some of his subjects sent to Ravensbruck, where he fled to. He then continued his sterilization studies. Soon, however, he ran again, this time to Schleswig-Holstein, to be with Himmler. he was the only Auschwitz doctor to be with Himmler in the end. On June 8, 1945, Clauberg was captured by allied forces.

EVIL AGENDA OF THE SECRET GOVERNMENT

He was sent to the Soviet Gulag for three years before being tried. Once tried, he was convicted of war crimes and sentenced to another 25 years. On August 9, 1945, he was found dead in his prison cell.

DOCTOR JOHANN PAUL KREMER

Doctor Johann Paul Kremer was one of the oldest doctors in the camps. Kremer was already 59 when he began work at Auschwitz. He had previously been a professor of anatomy at the University of Munster. He was the only professor to be appointed an SS camp doctor. Although he was a professor, he was never given his own laboratory, which always upset him.

Dr. Kremer, while at the University of Munster, was extremely interested in the problems and pathways of starvation. This heavily influenced his research at Auschwitz. He chose patients that were already selected for death in the gas chambers. He made them lay on a table and began an in depth questionnaire about the subject's weight and weight loss patterns. Kremer would then order his assistant to inject phenol into the subject's heart.

Kremer noted that, "I [Kremer] stood at a distance from the dissection table holding jars, ready for the segments [organs] cut out immediately after death...segments of the liver, spleen and pancreas." Kremer had a strong inclination towards anything unusual. It is reported that when he saw someone whose head was interestingly shaped, he would order them to be photographed and injected for study. Although it was atypical for most Nazi doctors, Kremer was known for keeping an exacting diary. His diary covered many themes, including his "victimization by the medical establishment."

It is now known the reason that Kremer was so intent on collecting organs immediately after death was because he used them to conduct research on a theory he had hypothesized earlier. His theory was that phagocytes (cells which attack foreign agents), specifically white blood cells, are really degenerated organ tissues. By collecting "fresh" organs, Kremer could continue his research.

Dr. Kremer, however, was best known around the camp, and indeed in the entire Nazi Doctor community, for his extreme detachment from the emotional side of his work. However, even Kremer was disgusted at times. At the end of the war Kremer was apprehended and sent to jail for 10 years in Poland. He was then tried in his home of Munster. He was sentenced to another ten years in jail, which was waived due to his service in Poland. Dr. Kremer died in 1965.

CHEMICAL WEAPONS RESEARCH

Little is known about the Mustard Gas experiments, and they are often termed the "lost" gas experiments. It is known, however, that at Sachsenhausen and Natzweiler, between September 1939 and April 1945, test with lost gas were conducted. Like Rascher's high altitude experiments, these results were to be used by the Luftwaffe to test effectiveness and severity of wounds. Many subjects died, and all of the others experienced extreme pain. At Nuremberg, Karl Brandt, Handloser, Blome, Rostock, Gebhardt, Rudolf Brandt, and Sievers were charged with conducting these tests.

SULFANILAMIDE

The sulfanilamide experiments were conducted at Ravensbruck (where many of the Auschwitz doctors fled) between July 1942 and September 1943. Again, these experiments were conducted to give results to the state. This specific set of tests was conducted for the benefit of the ground forces in Germany. Subjects were intentionally wounded, and these wounds were then infected with tetanus, gas gangrene and streptococcus.

EVIL AGENDA OF THE SECRET GOVERNMENT

The subject's blood vessels were then tied off, to simulate a war wound. This halted circulation. Glass and wood shavings were then placed into the wound to aggravate it further. The patients were then treated with sulfanilamide to test it's ability to cure such wounds. As in most other experiments, many subjects died. All other subjects suffered extreme pain, many losing limbs.

PHOSPHOROUS

The phosphorous/incendiary bomb experiments were conducted at the Buchenwald camp between November 1943 and January 1944. Phosphorous material from incendiary bombs was used to burn subject's skin. The physicians then tested a myriad of pharmaceutical solution on the wounds. Reports include severe pain, and extremely serious bodily injury.

POISON

The poison experiments were conducted at the Buchenwald camp between December 1943 and October 1944. These tests were extremely simple compared to others. Poison was put into subject's food, secretly. All patients died as a result. Some were left to die, and others were killed immediately so that the physicians could perform autopsies. Beginning in about September 1944, SS began shooting subjects with poisoned bullets.

REGENERATION

The regeneration experiments (bone, muscle, nerve, and bone transplant) were conducted at the Ravensbruck camp between September 1942 and December 1943. As with most of the wartime experiments, the results of these tests were to be used by the Luftwaffe. Segments of bone, nerve and muscle were transferred from one subject to the next. Most subjects became permanently debilitated and/or mutilated. It has also been recently reported that the first attempts at cloning were attempted at this time. Fortunately, all cloning experiments apparently failed. However, there were successful experiments with human/primate breeding that resulted in the births of over a dozen chimpanzee/human hybrids. These creatures were destined to become slaves, but were destroyed by Nazi scientists as Allied troops advanced into Germany.

SEA WATER

The sea water experiments were conducted at the Dachau camp between July 1944 and September 1944. Again, these tests were to benefit the Luftwaffe and the Navy, in attempt to make sea water potable. Procedurally, subjects were starved and given only sea water that had been chemically altered in numerous ways. These tests caused extreme pain and permanent damage to the subjects.

JAUNDICE

The epidemic jaundice experiments were conducted at Sachsenhausen and Natzweiler between June 1943 and January 1945. Again, these tests were conducted for the benefit of the Luftwaffe, to search for a vaccine against epidemic jaundice. The subjects were infected with jaundice and attempts were made to cure them with various agents. Extreme pain, and commonly death, were the final results of these tests.

The debate continues concerning the discoveries made by Nazi scientific research. Many believe that the discoveries made by the horrific experiments should never be studied and used due to the innocent lives lost in the process of discovery. Others feel that using the research could benefit millions of people, thereby bringing some kind of meaning to the millions of lives snuffed out all for the sake of scientific curiosity.

EVIL AGENDA OF THE SECRET GOVERNMENT

Even women and children were rounded up for
unholy scientific experiments conducted by
Nazi "doctors" and "scientists."

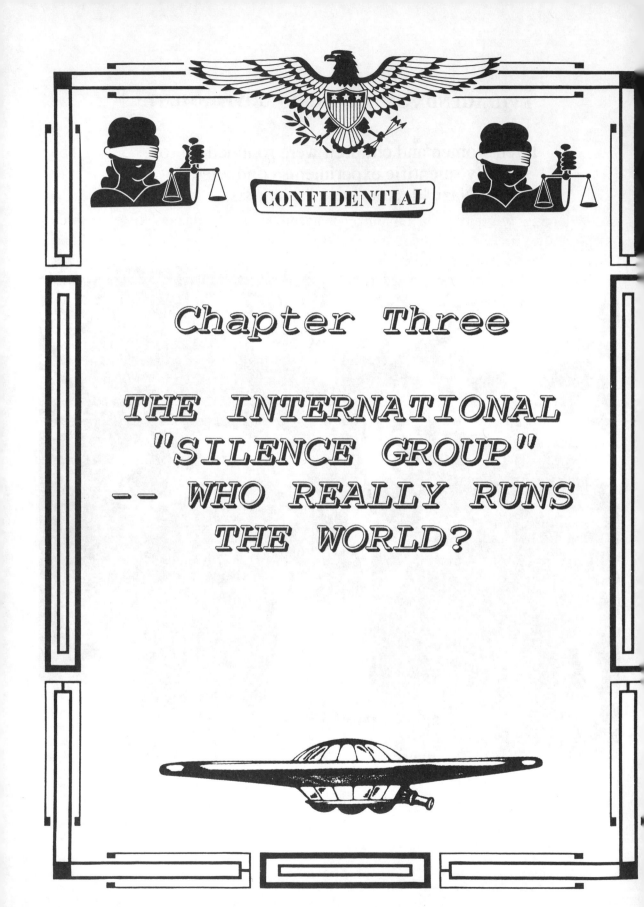

CONFIDENTIAL

Chapter Three

THE INTERNATIONAL "SILENCE GROUP" -- WHO REALLY RUNS THE WORLD?

EVIL AGENDA OF THE SECRET GOVERNMENT

THE SECRET GROUP

According to former British Intelligence agent Dr. John Coleman, there are three major groups in the world today that secretly controls vast amounts of political and financial power. The Secret groups - the Wicca-Masons, the Maltese-Jesuits and the Dark-Nobility all work for and under the central Bavarian Command, or the Bavarian Illuminati, which binds them all together.

The Bavarians created the Bilderberg society for the purpose of world control, the core of which contains a council of 13 members from each of the three groups, or 39 in all. The old-line ruling families who believe that they have the right to rule the world because they are descended from the emperors of the ancient Roman and so-called "Holy Roman Empires" consist of some 13- 15 "blue blood" families. Some of these families include: Rothschilds, Kuhn, Loeb, Lehman, Rockefeller, Sachs, Warburg, Lazard, Seaf, Goldman, Schiff, Morgan, Schroeder, Bush, Harriman.

The Bavarian Illuminati and its Nazi connections calls for the establishment of a National Socialist World Government. The secret roots of the World Socialist movement in all its forms can also be traced back to Bavaria, Germany, and the secret societies there to which Mazzini, Marx and Lenin had close ties. The target date for a full Nazi takeover is the year 2000, with an "incubation period" for their New World Order being 1995-2000. It is believed by some that the Nazi's, may use neutron bombs that have been placed in strategic positions in major cities as a means of "nuclear blackmail" if their "Global 2000" coup d'etat does not come off as planned.

A I.T.N. World News Broadcast out of London made a brief mention in early 1995 of a plane that had been intercepted en-route from Moscow to Frankfurt, Germany. The plane carried a shipment of weapons-grade plutonium, and the rumors were that the Bavarian Secret Service had created a nuclear black market in the former Soviet

EVIL AGENDA OF THE SECRET GOVERNMENT

Union and were smuggling plutonium into Germany for some unknown purpose. This report appeared once, yet strangely there were few follow-up reports in later broadcasts, and certainly nothing was reported in the American media.

This may not be the first time that the Third Reich has used nuclear blackmail on the United States. According to author William P. Lyne in his book, ***Space Aliens from the Pentagon***: ***Flying Saucers Are Man-Made Electrical Machines***, Lyne maintains that the Germans tested a neutron bomb in 1931 in the Libyan desert, and that during World War II threatened the United States with destruction unless it provided the Nazi's with a safe haven. If Operation Paperclip is any indication, the blackmail apparently worked.

The secret plan of the Nazi's New World Order is to impose on this planet a centralized world fascist state in which there will be genocide on a massive scale. There will be total state control over all aspects of human behavior with complete control of the human mind and spirit. This will be accomplished through manipulation of the world's major religions, genetic engineering, drugs, and a tightly-controlled media. There will be death camps in which "undesirable" races, the old and infirm, and those without "social utility" will be exterminated. The institution of state-sanctioned slavery will be reestablished. There will no longer be families as we know them today. There will be a Master Race in charge of all this power, augmented by advanced genetics, and bred for superior characteristics. Their target date is the coming second millennium, the year 2000.

During WW II the Bavarian Illuminati, or the Secret Group, arranged through the German war machine to loot the treasuries of Austria, Belgium, Czechoslovakia, The Netherlands, and the gold and jewels once owned by murdered Jews. Reinhard Gehlen oversaw the "Odessa" operation from 1942-45 in which most of the currency, stolen art, and gold was shipped by various means to Argentina. The missing gold alone, in pre-1939 dollars, was worth at least $600 million.

HE'S WATCHING YOU

EVIL AGENDA OF THE SECRET GOVERNMENT

Since then, the Bavarian Illuminati has used the bullion cache as credit for its operations, including economic warfare against the United States. In addition, a good part of the secret funding over the years has come from large-scale diversions of funds from all major treasuries in the western world. The principal method involves diverting cash credits for funds coming into the government through the Secret Group's control of central banks like the Federal Reserve. The "skim" appears to be about .5% of all incoming funds. A significant portion of the diverted funds go to campaign funds for members of Congress as "protection." Because of this, no one in the Government has much interest in looking into the diversion. Even those in Congress who are "clean" are typically co-opted by promises of more power or are just silenced.

This secret has been a carefully-planned fifty-year war. The late 40s and 50s were spent putting their agents in place and rebuilding their main client's European industrial base with American money. The initial steps in the American overthrow occurred in the 1960's through several of the Group's most critical agents, Earl Warren and LBJ, with assists from J. Edgar Hoover and others.

One of the first things the Group did to protect its own covert operation was one of Reinhard Gehlen's specialties in WW II Nazi intelligence, divert attention to the "Red menace." What the Secret Group wanted by the time of the "incubation period" (1995-2000), was a society that was uneducated, amoral, uncommitted to democratic institutions, living in fear, with a sudden and drastic reduction in spendable income simultaneous with societal chaos. The Secret Group thought that this could produce the environment for rejection of the democratic form of government that they seek by 2000.

In the 1960s the Secret Group's agents started the process of eliminating religious and moral ideals from American life, particularly in the schools. They removed as many impediments to criminality as they could get away with, dramatically increased media (TV), portrayal of violence and joblessness, reduced the standards of education and early training for rational thought and fostered every possible dislocation in family structure they could engineer.

EVIL AGENDA OF THE SECRET GOVERNMENT

The plan is to unleash elemental forces of chaos that transcend government philosophy. The primitive mandate for political/social structure seems to be protection of the person from crime and disease, protection of property, a system of justice to enforce those protection, and organization for economic gain. All these refinements we've developed, democracy, fascism, communism, monarchy, all come after the primitive mandates have been met. The theory is that if you remove enough of those basic protections, the government will fall because it is not performing the more important, elementary functions.

BIOLOGICAL WARFARE AND DRUGS

The mystery of deadly, newly emerging diseases has confounded scientists as to the origins and rapid development of such pathogens. Evidence suggests that diseases like AIDS were man-made and deliberately introduced into certain population groups. The Secret Group reportedly developed the AIDS virus principally at Albert Ludwigs University in Freiburg im Brisgau. The London Times reported on May 5, 1987 the theory that the AIDs epidemic was man-made and connected with the World Health Organization's smallpox eradication program in Africa.

According to Dr. Peter Piot, executive director of the Joint United Nations Program on HIV/AIDS, or UNAIDS, in 1997, more than 20 million people in sub-Saharan Africa carry the virus that causes AIDS, and most of them don't even know it. It has also been suggested that AIDS was introduced to the United States in 1978-79 with the hepatitis B vaccine experiments among homosexuals on the west coast.

The Secret Group chose homosexuals because they believed that few people would care what happened to them and hoped the disease would spread throughout the country before anyone realized that it could kill anyone, not just gays. During the "incubation period" (1995-2000), the Secret Group plans to introduce new diseases that will be "far more aggressive, far more vicious" than AIDS or other "natural diseases."

41

EVIL AGENDA OF THE SECRET GOVERNMENT

Crime and illegal drugs go hand-in-hand. Drug traffic has been fostered under the covert aegis of the Secret Group's massive apparatus within the CIA since at least Vietnam. CIA operatives under control of the Secret Group were running hard drugs from Laos and Cambodia to Bien Hoa to the United States. These shipments were smuggled aboard military aircraft and ships for use on American streets. It went on for years and is probably still going on, now from other points of origin. There are also alliances between the Secret Group's agents in CIA and the military and drug lords in South America. The whole government sponsored "war on drugs" is actually a profit-making venture in order to fund various illegal activities around the world.

Illegal drugs command high prices on the black market. If the illegality of drugs is taken away, then so is the huge amounts of money and profits. Law-enforcement on the local level are also not interested in making controlled substances legal, but not for the reasons put forth by the media. If drugs are made legal, crime would actually drop since the large amounts of money commanded for drugs would be gone. Local law-enforcement, through forfeiture laws, are able to legally steal money and property from "suspected" drug dealers and users, providing capital to finance the hidden agenda. As long as there is money to be made, drugs will remain illegal and profitable for the Secret Group.

The Secret Group's plan is to covertly foster and finance a civil war on race lines through their agents in black and Hispanic ghettoes in major cities. Once they are successful in gun control legislation, the Secret Group will arm the minority insurgents with attack weapons to be used against essentially weapon-less minority and non-minority individuals. The local police departments will be out-gunned. The military will be called in, but will be unable to control the situation due to an artificial "breakdown in the chain of command."

In the midst of the chaos, after the war begins, the Group will conduct systematic assassinations of key American civilian and military leaders who have not supported the Group's policies or its key agents. The civil war fostered covertly by the Group will

EVIL AGENDA OF THE SECRET GOVERNMENT

frighten "middle America" into adoption of the Group's government. After the year 2000 the civil war will be used by the Group as the excuse for genocide against the African and Hispanic races. Literally hundreds of smaller races also targeted. This will take place over a much longer period than the German experiment before and during World War II.

The current scaling back of civil right laws in the United States has been covertly funded by the Secret Group. Most politicians on the local, state and national level have been all too willing to pass laws limiting our basic human dignities, that is if enough money is funneled into their pockets. The Secret Group in order to continue their hidden agenda has plenty of money to spend on greedy politicians.

While a lot of people in the United States have been all too willing to accept the new era of "hate" rhetoric concerning homosexuals, minority groups, single mothers and the poor. Others have realized that there is a more sinister influence at work in the world today. An influence that has control of the highest levels of the country's political and military infrastructure.

SURVIVAL AFTER THE WAR

A Reuters News service press release dated May 10, 1996 seems to confirm that the Nazis intended to continue with their secret agenda, even after the fall of Germany in 1945. The article stated that the Nazis, realizing they were losing the war in 1944, met with top German industrialists to plan a secret post- war international network to restore them to power. High level Nazi government and intelligence officials also secretly met with a number of world leaders in an attempt to "save their own skins." These meetings were extremely successful with certain South American countries who shared in the Nazis ideology. This was according to a recently declassified U.S. intelligence document.

EVIL AGENDA OF THE SECRET GOVERNMENT

As Nazis storm Europe, German troops
roam the streets. Look closely and you will
see what appears to be a demonic face laughing
at the antics of Hitler's unholy army.

44

EVIL AGENDA OF THE SECRET GOVERNMENT

The document, which appears to confirm a meeting historians have long argued about, says an SS general and a representative of the German armaments ministry told such companies as Krupp and Roehling that they must be prepared to finance the Nazi party after the war when it went underground. They were also told: "Existing financial reserves in foreign countries must be placed at the disposal of the party so that a strong German empire can be created after the defeat."

The document, detailing an August 1944 meeting, was obtained from the World Jewish Congress, which has been working with the Senate Banking Committee and the Holocaust Museum to determine what happened to looted Jewish money and property in the Second World War. As a result of the probe, thousands of documents from "Operation Safehaven" have been made public. The operation was a U.S. intelligence effort to track how the German government used Swiss banks during the war to hide looted Jewish assets.

The three-page document, released by the National Archives, was sent from Supreme Headquarters of the Allied Expeditionary Force to the U.S. secretary of state in November 1944. It described a secret meeting at the Maison Rouge in Strasbourg, occupied France, on August 10, 1944. The source for the report was an agent who attended and "had worked for the French on German problems since 1916."

Jeffrey Bale, a Columbia University expert on clandestine Nazi networks, said historians have debated whether such a meeting could have taken place because it came a month after the attempt on Adolf Hitler's life, which had led to a crackdown on discussions of a possible German military defeat. Bale said the Red House meeting was mentioned in Nazi hunter Simon Wiesenthal's 1967 book, *The Murderers Among Us*, and again in a 1978 book by French Communist Victor Alexandrov, *The SS Mafia*.

A U.S. Treasury Department analysis in 1946 reported that the Germans had transferred $500 million out of the country before the war's end to countries such as

EVIL AGENDA OF THE SECRET GOVERNMENT

Spain, Switzerland, Lichtenstein, Portugal, Argentina and Turkey, where it was used to buy hundreds of companies. The intelligence document further stated: "As soon as the Nazi party becomes strong enough to re-establish its control over Germany, the industrialists will be paid for their efforts and cooperation by concessions and orders."

The meeting was presided over by a "Dr Scheid," described as an SS Obergruppenfuhrer (general) and director of Hermsdorff & Schonburg Company. Attending were representatives of seven German companies including Krupp, Roehling, Messerschmidt, and Volkswagenwerk and officials of the ministries of armaments and the navy. The industrialists were from companies with extensive interests in France. Scheid was quoted as saying the battle of France was lost and "from now, German industry must realize that the war cannot be won and it must take steps in preparation for a post-war commercial campaign." He said German industry must make contacts and alliances with foreign firms and lay the groundwork for borrowing considerable sums in foreign countries.

Scheid cited the Krupp company's sharing of patents with U.S. companies so that they would have to work with Krupp. A representative of the armaments ministry then presided over a smaller second meeting with Scheid and representatives of Krupp and Roehling, who were told the war was lost and would continue only until the unity of Germany was guaranteed. He said they must prepare themselves to finance the Nazi party when it went underground. The intelligence report added that the meetings signaled a new Nazi policy "whereby industrialists with government assistance will export as much of their capital as possible."

Sybil Milton, senior historian at Washington's Holocaust Museum, said it has long been known that the Nazis planned to do something after the war and the document's importance may be in pointing researchers in a direction where they could determine what had been done. "Now that the Nazi secret plan has been confirmed, the central question is whether it has been carried out," said Elan Steinberg, executive director of the World Jewish Congress. Amongst their contacts in the United States, the Nazi "elite" could rely on the generous assistance of a well-connected patron, Pedro Del Valle, who went on to become a vice president of ITT.

In 1954, Del Valle, a retired Marine Corps lieutenant general, was soundly defeated in his run for the Republican nomination. His campaign was spiced with public endorsements of a Anti-Semitic tract called *Know Your Enemy*. Twenty years later, Del Valle and ITT consultant John McCone, formerly a CIA director, threw in to overthrow Allende in Chile's 1970 elections. ITT funneled $350,000 into the event, and when the brutal dictatorship of Pinochet was installed, the conglomerate conspired with other politically "conservative" companies to pirate the country's natural resources.

As a hedge against the fall of the Third Reich, German industrialists had made provisions in 1944 for protecting their loot from confiscation by the U.S. and England. Under the instruction of Martin Bormann, the surviving SS, soon to be known as ODESSA, established hundreds of corporations abroad, donated handsomely to extreme right-wing political candidates in the U.S. and cleared the path for the reconstruction of the Reich on foreign soil. All of this was accomplished by channeling the loot through a labyrinth of secret bank accounts to non-belligerent countries, and under Bormann's direction, financed 750 news companies worldwide to direct the Nazi Party reconstruction.

Over 100 of those companies were based in the United States. Funds mysteriously appeared in the bank accounts of Germany's agents around the world. They were instructed to invest in selected businesses, propaganda mills in the U.S. and elsewhere, give legal aid to indicted Nazis, purchase out-of-the-way estates for Nazi leaders in foreign countries, and so on. These funds also supported the "rat lines," escape routes from the Allied advance set up every 40 miles along the German border. These well planed routes allowed thousands of Nazis to flee Europe along with their stolen assets.

EVIL AGENDA OF THE SECRET GOVERNMENT

Fascist opinion in the United States was carried along by American contacts. **For America**, a spin-off of the America First Committee, was formed in 1954, ran by some of the leading World War II "isolationists." One of the organization's leaders was Colonel Robert McCormick, publisher of the *Chicago Tribune*. The chairman of For America was Clarence Manion, formerly dean of law at Notre Dame University. Manion once sat on Eisenhower's Commission on Inter-Governmental Affairs.

The stated aim of **For America** was the support of political candidates sympathetic to the Nazi cause. Three congressmen made up the recruiting arm of the organization: Burton K. Wheeler, Hamilton Fish and Howard Buffett. Hamilton Fish, a Republican Party leader, had as his greatest ambition the start of a third party based on principles of National Socialism. The others were already in disrepute for involvement in "non-interventionist" America First chapters and other enclaves of domestic Nazism during the war.

Confiscated Jewish assets were routed into the Nazi rebirth and turned up in the most unusual places. On September 20, 1996, a half century after the fact, the Associated Press noted: "Tons of gold looted by Nazis during World War II, some of it possibly taken from the fillings in Holocaust victims' teeth, are stored in the Federal Reserve Bank of New York and the Bank of England in London.

Recently declassified federal documents show that six tons of gold looted by Nazis are stored in the two banks, the World Jewish Congress said. The group's president has written to the two countries asking that the gold be returned to Holocaust survivors." Elan Steinberg, speaking for the World Jewish Congress, based his allegations on declassified State Department documents that confirm two tons of Nazi gold had turned up in New York vaults (worth about $28 million) and four tons ($56 million) in London. There is the feeling that this gold is simply a "drop in the bucket" considering the billions of dollars worth of gold, jewelry, artwork and other assets that have disappeared completely after the fall of the Third Reich.

Is the New World Order preparing to launch an all out war on humankind?

EVIL AGENDA OF THE SECRET GOVERNMENT

In 1997, reporter Stan Lehman revealed that two safe deposit boxes were opened in Sao Paulo, Brazil. The contents, a $4 million dollar fortune, had possibly been stolen from Jews by the Nazis during World War II.

The boxes, locked up for more than 14 years in the government-owned Banco de Brasil in San Paulo, contained 230 items, including rubies, sapphires, emeralds, gold fillings and dental crowns, and $12,125 in cash. Also enclosed was a passport issued by the Third Reich to the man who left behind the fortune: Albert Blume, a German citizen who arrived in Brazil in 1938 and died in 1983.

Witnessing the opening of the two safety boxes were members of a government commission investigating whether fugitive Nazis brought looted Jewish wealth to Brazil. For them, the most important item found was Blume's diary with entries written in German.

"The diary will tell us who Blume's comrades were," said Henry Sobel, a senior rabbi at Sao Paulo's Jewish Congregation. "It will also tell us how the Nazi network functioned in Brazil." Sobel, a member of the investigative commission, said he read parts of the diary which "prove that Blume was a member of the Nazi party and of the army of the Third Reich."

"There are many unanswered questions in this thriller, like who was Blume? What was he doing in Brazil and what kind of help did he and other Nazis receive from the Brazilian government to establish themselves in this country?" Sobel said.

After World War II, many Nazis sought a safe haven in Brazil and Argentina, where they found vast spaces, communities of German immigrants and sympathetic, authoritarian leaders. About 1,500 Nazis entered Brazil after the war, Sobel said.

EVIL AGENDA OF THE SECRET GOVERNMENT

Among the war criminals who fled to Brazil were Josef Mengele, the "angel of death" of the Auschwitz extermination camp, who lived quietly in Sao Paulo until his death in 1979.

The daunting task now facing the commission is to determine if Blume's fortune was plundered from Jews or, as some have claimed, was the result of Blume's work as a pawnbroker. If it belonged to Jews then it "must be returned to the rightful owners or their descendants," Sobel said.

Ricardo Penteado, a court-appointed lawyer who has investigated the case for 10 years, said, "I cannot categorically state that Blume was a Nazi or that his fortune once belonged to Jews." Penteado, who was present at the opening of the safety boxes, said interviews with Blume's relatives in the southern Brazilian state of Santa Catarina "indicate that he fled Germany to escape Nazi persecution of homosexuals."

Many of the items in the safe, he added, were made well after World War II, "and there is evidence that Blume acquired them while working as a pawnbroker." He said there were documents showing that Blume joined the Nazi party in 1935 and was kicked out one year later.

Blume, a bachelor, had no outward signs of wealth. He lived alone in a tiny one-bedroom apartment in downtown Sao Paulo, Penteado said. Although several people have tried to claim Blume's fortune using forged wills, Penteado said Blume's only heir is a 94-year-old aunt who lives in Joinville, 330 miles southwest of Sao Paulo.

No one knows the exact amount of the Third Reich's plundered wealth. Nor is there any good explanation on what has happened to much of it. The possibility exists that this capital is being used today to continue funding the eventual rebirth of the Nazi empire.

Chapter Four

THE THIRD REICH'S QUEST FOR POWER AND THE DISCOVERY OF ATOMIC FISSION

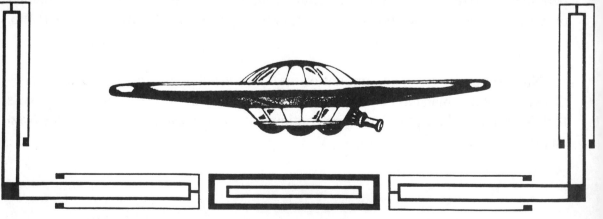

EVIL AGENDA OF THE SECRET GOVERNMENT

In December of 1938 an experiment by German physicist Otto Hahn led to the discovery of atomic fission. In the following months, physicists around the world realized Hahn's discovery could lead to a successful chain-reacting uranium pile. The theoretical possibility of a super-explosive, an atomic bomb, was closer to becoming a reality.

In June of 1942 Churchill and Roosevelt met in Washington D.C. to discuss the issue of "Tube Alloys," the code name for the atomic bomb. It was agreed that German nuclear research was probably ahead of the Western Allies by as much as two years. The Germans had stopped exporting uranium from Czechoslovakia and had been furthering their research with a substance called "heavy water." Heavy water, sometimes called deterium oxide, is unique because it contains atoms of double atomic weight. This characteristic slows down neutrons in uranium 235 and effectively creates a chain reaction of exploding atoms, the basis of the atomic bomb.

Heavy water is created with enormous amounts of electrical power. During the war there was only one hydro-electric plant in the world capable of creating large amounts of this substance, and that was the Norsk Hydro plant at Vemork, Norway, a country occupied by the Nazis since 1940. Churchill and Roosevelt agreed to pool their countries' efforts in nuclear research. However, neither country had developed a large enough supply of heavy water, so research would be done with a graphite-uranium pile instead of the uranium-heavy water pile used by the Germans. In case the graphite method proved fruitless a heavy water plant was to be built in British Columbia.

MI6 Director Stewart Menzies put Lt. Cmdr. Welsh, the chief of the Norwegian country section of MI6, in charge of a commando attack on the Vemork plant. Welsh was convinced he could find a way to destroy or cripple the plant. Though many Norwegian scientists had fled Norway when the Nazis took control, Professor Leif Tronstad, designer and construction supervisor of the Vemork plant, stayed in Norway and sent to London a large amount of industrial information about the German's intentions of increasing production of heavy water at the Norsk plant.

EVIL AGENDA OF THE SECRET GOVERNMENT

His activities were unfortunately cut short in September of 1942 when a double agent informed Tronstad that the Nazis were aware of his illegal transmissions. Tronstad reluctantly left his family and country and escaped to Great Britain.

In October of 1941 the underground secret intelligence service in Denmark alarmed MI6 when they sent a telegram outlining the details of a meeting between Danish physicist and a German scientist Werner Heisenber. The conversation led the Danish physicist to believe that the Nazis were close to developing the ultimate weapon, the atomic bomb.

Tronstad was made head of Section IV of the Norwegian High Command in London. He was in charge of intelligence espionage and sabotage, but none of his activities were as important as his communication with his friend and colleague Dr. Jomar Brun, the chief manager of production at the Vemork plant. Tronstad wished to establish a line of communication with his old friend.

The contact was made when six of Tronstad's men, all Norwegian natives, were parachuted onto the Hardanger plateau near Vemork, March 29, 1942. Head of the mission was Einar Skinnarland who had excellent knowledge of the area. Skinnarland was successful in contacting Brun. Tronstad and Brun exchanged messages by secret writings through Stockholm.

Tronstad wondered if it were possible to transport a large amount of heavy water to London by landing a British plane on a frozen lake near Vemork, but Brun felt it was impossible. Brun began to sabotage the production of the heavy water by adding cod-liver oil to the water. This stopped production for several days at a time. Brun and Skinnarland collected photos, drawings of the countryside as well as specific details about the plant. They microfilmed this data, concealed it in toothpaste tubes, and had the tubes delivered to Tronstad via Sweden.

EVIL AGENDA OF THE SECRET GOVERNMENT

Was the development of the V-2 rocket merely a "front" for more advanced technology operating on magnetic principles?

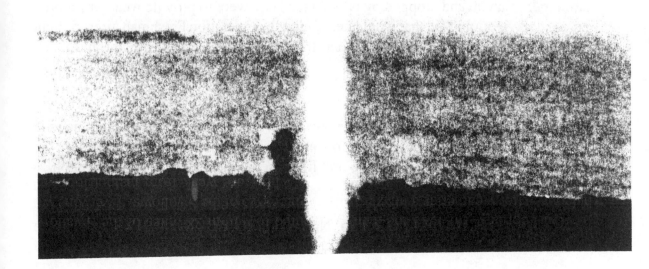

EVIL AGENDA OF THE SECRET GOVERNMENT

MI6 studied the information. Menzies approached the Joint Intelligence Committee with a proposition that the Vemork plant be destroyed as soon as possible. Quickly plans were made to send a commando team of paratroopers into Norway. The plan was called **Operation Freshman**. Thirty-four commandos of the First Airborne Division were to land in two Horsa gliders on the Hardanger plateau and then proceed by bicycle to the plant. They were to kill the German guards on the suspension bridge that led across a gorge to the plant. After they destroyed machinery and stocks of heavy water they were to split into groups of no more than three and make their way to Sweden. If possible they were to bring back any of the 200 cubic centimeter steel flasks of heavy water that they could manage.

There was doubt that the mission could be successful. Many reasons were cited by Tronstad - Norway's terrain was not suitable for glider landings, weather was harsh and unpredictable, the folding bicycles would prove to be worthless in the event of snowfall and the men were expected to travel 400 miles to the Swedish border.

Bombing the plant was an option, but Tronstad opposed this also. If the plant's liquid storage tanks were hit the entire Rjukan population could be in grave danger. On October 18, 1942 four Norwegians led by Jens Poulsson were flown over the Hardanger plateau and dropped by parachute. They were to provide weather reports, operate a navigational aid that would help guide the Operation Freshman aircraft, light up the landing area with beacons, guide the troops to the Vemork plant and make reports by a portable telegraph unit.

Tronstad ordered Brun to leave Norway. Brun reluctantly agreed. He and his wife carried two kilos of heavy water and poison ampules in case they were caught by the Nazis. They traveled by train to Oslo and from there were safely flown to London.

The day the Bruns left for London, November 9, 1942, the Poulsson team made contact with Tronstad and London. After great hardship they had made their way to an abandoned cabin on the plateau and reported among other things that the navigational aid had been tested and was operating correctly. As the Norwegian telegraph operator made his report the London operator grew suspicious. Every operator has an individual style of manipulating the sending key. These idiosyncrasies were known as the operator's fingerprints and a record was made of them for security reasons. As the Norwegian operated his sending key, with fingers numb with cold, the London operator recognized an unfamiliar pattern and thought the Gestapo had captured the sending station.

The London operator made security checks, and the Norwegian replied satisfactorily. There was one final question that had to be answered with a previously agree upon answer. "What did you see walking down the Strand in the early hours of January 1, 1941?" The Norwegian replied with the correct answer, "Three pink elephants." MI6 in London knew all was well.

November 19, 1942 the commandos of Operation Freshman, all volunteers in their early twenties, boarded two Horsa gliders at Wick airfield in Scotland. Those at MI6 that were skeptical the mission would be successful had their reservations confirmed. The second tandem of plane and glider both crashed. All four men were killed on the Halifax plane. German troops reached the crash site of the glider the next morning in the mountains northeast of Helleland, Norway. There were fourteen surviving commandos. The Nazis interrogated them and then followed a recent edict by Hitler that "crews of sabotage planes are to be shot." The Germans executed the commandos by firing squad.

The first Halifax-Horsa tandem made its landing site where Poulsson's team heard the Halifax overhead. But the Halifax crew didn't realize where they were and had to turn back toward the proposed site. By the time the Halifax crew realized they had over-shot their target they decided to return to Scotland since there was only enough fuel to do just that. The planes began picking up ice and the towline snapped. The Halifax crew radioed London that the Horsa glider had plunged into the sea, but actually the glider had crashed into the mountains near Lyse Fjord. Eight were killed in the crash. The others were taken to Wehrmacht and Gestapo headquarters for interrogation. When it was found that they were too injured to be of any use they were poisoned by a German medical officer. When a map with Vemork circled in ink was found there was no question as to the mission of the men. The five remaining men were all shot.

The glider disaster was a hard blow to MI6. Col. Jack Wilson, the chief of Norwegian Section, had always been against the glider mission, but felt they had a good change with paratroopers. He selected Norwegian Lt. Joachim Ronneberg to select five expert skiers from the Royal Norwegian Army`s volunteers. They were to join Poulsson and his men (now code-named the Swallows) on the plateau. This second attack was named Operation Gunnerside.

Now MI6 was in the services of Dr. Brun who had built a model of the plant. He was able to answer most of the questions from the commandos about details of the plant. The commandos were trained at a special school in Scotland. The objective was to link up with the Swallows, and proceed to the plant. When they reached the plant they were to destroy the eighteen stainless steel cells of heavy water.

On February 16, 1943 the men parachuted to within 28 miles of the Swallow's hideout. After weathering a blizzard they sighted two of the Swallows. Everyone was in poor condition, especially the Swallows who were weak from malnutrition and hobbled with frost bite. The Gunnerside party began planning the attack. The only way to get into the plant without alerting the guards would be a dangerous descent into a gorge in front of the plant. Then they would climb a 500 foot face of the outcrop that the plant was built on.

On the evening of February 27 the nine men skied to the plant and descended into the gorge. They crossed the stream and began the difficult climb up the gorge. They reached the top about midnight, crept through a minefield and avoided the German guards. Two men entered the basement of the plant by crawling through a cable duct and then unlocked a door. There was only one workman in the plant, a Norwegian. The commandos, dressed in British uniforms, laid the charges on the eighteen cells that produced the heavy water. They set the fuses and told the workman to find safety on one of the upper floors.

All nine commandos left the plant and scrambled down the gorge, and as they did the charges went off destroying the cells. The Germans never saw the commandos until they were on the other side of the gorge. All escaped the German pursuit by skiing through a fierce blizzard. Two of the commandos stayed on the Hardanger plateau and the others skiied 250 miles to Sweden.

The mission was a complete success. It took the Germans six months to get the plant in good enough condition to produce heavy water again. On November 16, 1943, the American high command ordered the 8th Air Force to bomb the plant. The plant was sufficiently damaged to convince Goering, minister of the German atomic program, to move the heavy water production form Vemork to Germany.

Skinnarland radioed this information to London in November. At the end of January 1944 Skinnarland found that the Germans were going to transport approximately 14 tones of heavy water in various forms of concentration. The heavy water was stored in drums marked "Potlash Lye." The Germans began to transport them by rail. Knut Haukelid, a member of the Gunnerside operation, and Alf Larsen, the chief engineer at Vemork, planned a way of sabotaging the transportation. Larsen had found that the Germans were to ferry the load across Lak Tinnsjo in its journey to Germany. Haukelid made a journey on the ferry and concluded that it could be sunk if explosives blew a hole in the bow about forty-five minutes into the journey. He figured a plastique charge of 18 pounds would sink the ferry but leave the passengers as unharmed as possible.

EVIL AGENDA OF THE SECRET GOVERNMENT

On February 19, 1944 the night before the shipment was to arrive, Haukelid and two of his men set the charge with an electronic detonator and timed fuse. It was set for 10:45 AM The next morning SS guards helped transport the shipment onto the ferry and by 10 AM the ferry left with fifty-three passengers. Forty-five minutes later an explosion rocked the ferry and in five minutes the ferry, the railway wagons went to the bottom of the lake. Twenty-six passengers were drowned. Only three canisters were salvaged.

While it was hoped that this would put an end to the Third Reich's quest for atomic weapons, intelligence sources continued to report on further developments with Nazi atomic bomb research. By the end of the war, enough material to build two atomic bombs had been secretly transported out of Europe into South America. From that point the trail grew cold, leading some to believe that somewhere in the world today, someone still possesses atomic material for possible future use.

CONFIDENTIAL

Chapter Five

FACT OR FICTION? FOO-FIGHTERS, GHOST ROCKETS AND OTHER NAZI UFO TECHNOLOGY

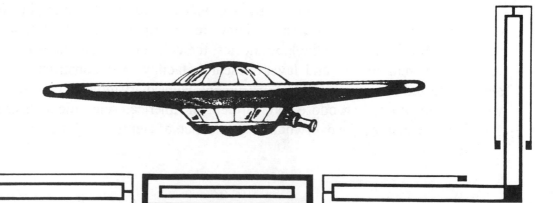

EVIL AGENDA OF THE SECRET GOVERNMENT

THE FOO - FIGHTERS

On November 27, 1944, a B-27 of the United States Air Force, returning from a raid on Speyer, West Germany, encountered a huge, orange colored light moving upward at an estimated speed of 500 MPH. The pilots reported the sighting, however, sector radar reported back that nothing was seen on the return screen. The strange object seen by the bomber was only the first of numerous others spotted by American pilots over wartime Europe.

The strange lights were baptized "Foo-fighters," taken from the then popular "Smokey Stover" comic strip. Further Allied encounters with foo fighters led experts to believe they were a new kind of German invention, employed to defeat radar. After the fall of Berlin, the Allies launched Operation Lusty to gather scientific papers, blueprints and experimental technology hidden away in abandoned mines, ancient castles, caves and buried vaults throughout occupied Europe.

In his review of Nazi technology, Colonel Donald Putt, assistant commanding officer for the Allied Technical Information Service (soon to serve in Operation Paperclip with a promotion to Lt. General), stated in July 1946 that fleeing German scientists had left behind, at Peenemunde, Wiener Neustadt (home of the "Foo-Fighters"), and elsewhere, prototypical marvels of future air warfare.

After the occupation of Germany, Colonel Putt toured the once-bustling R&D complex at Volkenrode. Journalist Tom Bower reported in 1987 that Putt was "amazed." Strolling though the laboratories, the colonel "realized he was in the midst of the most magnificent and lavish research facility ever constructed. The sheer abundance and extravagance of the instruments, subsidiary tools and testing equipment were awe-inspiring." Theodore von Karmen, an American scientific adviser to the Air Force, was struck by the overwhelming evidence of German technical superiority.

EVIL AGENDA OF THE SECRET GOVERNMENT

No one knows for certain who had the first
implant -- the Nazis, CIA or aliens; but
a number of these tiny objects have
recently been removed from indivduals
in various countries!

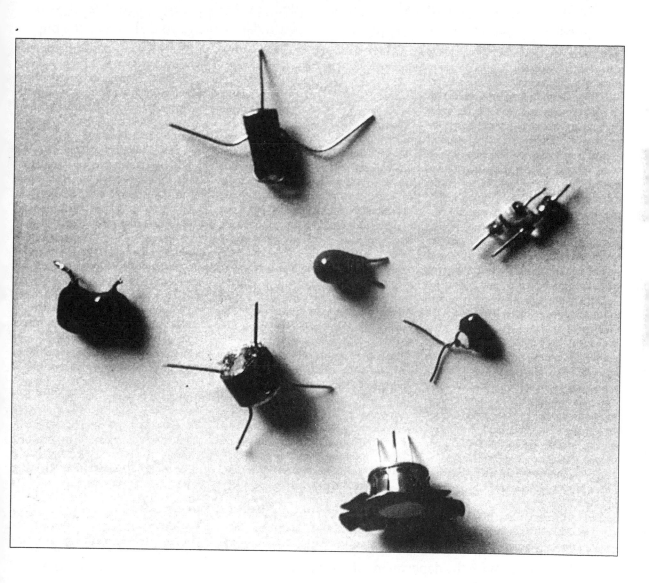

EVIL AGENDA OF THE SECRET GOVERNMENT

Seized German technical papers revealed that work on the German anti-radar Feurball, or fireball, had been sped up during the fall of 1944 at a Luftwaffe experimental center near Oberammergau, Bavaria. There, and at the aeronautical establishment at Weiner Neustadt, the first fireballs were produced. Later, when the Russians moved closer to Austria, the workshops producing the fireballs were moved to the Black Forest. Fast and remote controlled, the fireballs, equipped with klystron tubes, operated on the same frequency as Allied radar, which could eliminate the blips from radar screens. This allowed them to remain practically invisible to radar. The Nazi Feurball however, failed to interfere with the Allied air offensive.

The foo-fighters had been launched too late and could no longer change the course of events. However, they were significant not only because they were the outcome of a technical evolution which could have led to more dangerous weapons, but also because they showed that Nazi technology had moved in a direction far beyond anything expected by Allied Intelligence.

As the fall of Germany approached, the Nazi Leaders reverted to an ambitious project created by Gauleiter Franz Hofer who had become high commissioner for the Italian Tyrol and the Southern Alps. The project foresaw setting up an incredible fortress in the mountains, including parts of Italy, Austria and Bavaria. Hofer submitted his plan to Hitler's aide, Martin Bormann in November 1944, having prepared for this moment back in 1938 when Nazi agents carefully mapped all mountain passes, caves, bridges, highways, and located sights for underground factories, munitions dumps, arms and food caches.

To complete work on this fortress, Hofer demanded a slave labor force of a quarter of a million, to be composed of 70% Austrian workers and 30% men of the Tyrolese home guard. Vast workshops and launching pads were set up underground, among these were some 74 tunnels along Lake Garda, in Northern Italy, which were to be adapted and transformed into a vast assembly plant by FIAT of Turin in close collaboration with the department of Minister Albert Speer. Seven other tunnels along

EVIL AGENDA OF THE SECRET GOVERNMENT

Lake Garda, near Limone, were to produce several secret weapons systems tested at the Hermann Goering Institute of Riva del Garda.

According to the archives of the German High Command and of the Allied Combined Intelligence Objectives Sub-Committee, other plants in vital areas of Central Germany, code named M-Werke, were to produce powerful missiles such as the giant A-10 developed to destroy New York and Washington. Another report, never released by the Allies, and written by a French diplomat, mentioned the development of a strange gas that could knock aircraft out of the sky. The gas was based on the grisou (fire damp) gas found in mines, and which had been successfully tried against allied bombers over Lake Garda.

The contents of the diplomats report was no novelty to the Allies. Shortly after the bombing of Dresden, British and American intelligence had obtained a brief account concerning the use of some such weapon used against a group of twelve American bombers. That message, which came from an agent in Switzerland, also stated the attacker had been "a strange hemispherical object which flew at fantastic speeds and destroyed the bombers by expelling blue clouds of smoke or gas which disabled the bombers."

After the German surrender in May 1945, a team of British agents, investigating the files of some of the underground factories in the Black Forest, discovered that a large number of documents concerned experiments made with liquid oxygen for new turbine engines capable of developing extraordinary power. Other documents described the use of "gaseous explosives" which had been originally tested in Austria in 1936. Their existence was later confirmed by the ALSOS Mission and by Dr. Hans Friedrich Gold, of the Laboratory for Aeronautical Research at Volkenrode. The ejection of gas explosives had been part of the program tackled by researchers on Lake Garda and later tested with success by the circular flying object against Allied bombers. This object, in German military files, already had an operational name: "Round Lightning" (Kugelblitz).

EVIL AGENDA OF THE SECRET GOVERNMENT

German scientists had produced amazing improvements on the Feurball which, despite it's anti-radar effectiveness, remained comparatively harmless. However, by combining the principle of the aircraft with a round, symmetrical plane with direct gyroscopic stabilization, employing a total reaction turbine, adding remote control, vertical take off, infrared seeking equipment and electrostatic firing systems, the harmless Feurball became the lethal Kugelblitz. The "Round Lightning" weapon, the incredibly fast and mysterious disc-shaped craft that had been rumored and sighted in action, was used only once.

As the Allied forces crossed the Rhine, the only craft of it's type was destroyed by the SS on instructions from Berlin, to prevent it's capture. However, ever since, due to the severe censorship imposed by the "T" force of the British Army in Germany, and later, thanks to the complete blackout imposed by London, nothing more was heard of "Round Lightning."

According to writer Renato Vesco, Germany was sharing a great deal of the advances in weaponry with their allies the Japanese. In July of 1945, two and a half months after the war ended in Germany, a huge German transport submarine brought to Japan the latest of German inventions, two spherical wingless flying devices. The Japanese R&D team put the machines together, following the German instructions, which produced a ball shaped flying device without wings or propellers, however, nobody knew how it worked. The fuel was added, the start button of this unmanned machine was pressed and it disappeared with a roar and flames without a trace in the sky. The team never saw it again. The engineers were so frightened by the unexpected might of the machine, that they promptly dynamited the second prototype and chose to forget the whole incident.

THE SCHAUBERGER SAUCERS

One of the scientists reportedly involved with the early Nazi saucer projects was

EVIL AGENDA OF THE SECRET GOVERNMENT

Viktor Schauberger. Schauberger was an Austrian forester with a deep knowledge in biology, physics and chemistry. His sense and understanding on how water flows in the nature was exceptional. From his observations he formulated his hydrodynamic basic theory. Born towards the end of the nineteenth century in Austria, Schauberger's teacher was the natural world itself. In forests, alongside rivers, he studied the life-enhancing energy, which manifests in water or air as vortices.

"Prevailing technology uses the wrong forms of motion. It is based on entropy - on motions which nature uses to break down and scatter materials. However, Nature uses a different type of motion for creating order and new growth. The prevailing explosion-based technology - fuel burning and atom splitting - fills the world with expanding, heat-generating centrifugal motion."

Energy production, he believed, could instead use inward-moving, cold-generating centripetal motion, the same that nature employs to build and enliven substances. Even hydro-electric power plants, Schauberger said, use a destructive motion - they pressure water and chop it through turbines. The result is "dead water." He built suction turbines which enliven and invigorate, resulting in clean, life-giving water downstream. Schauberger produced electrical power from a unique suction turbine by implosion principles, and later was pressured into developing a propulsion system using the same principles applied to air.

After Hitler and the Nazis came into power, Schauberger's experiments started to attract attention. At one point Hitler threatened to hang Schauberger and his entire family if he did not co-operate with Nazi plans. Hitler wanted Schauberger to supervise the building of a new flying craft which levitated without burning any fuel. Because of the war, the Third Reich was desperate for new technological aid, but Schauberger did not want to give the Third Reich any technological advantages. He went to work as ordered, but deliberately took a great deal of time over everything, hoping to foil Hitler and his plans.

EVIL AGENDA OF THE SECRET GOVERNMENT

The idea of a new type of flying craft was based on Schauberger's discovery, made a few years earlier, of how to develop a low-pressure zone at the atomic level. He had actually achieved this in a laboratory, when his prototype whirled air or water "radically and axially" at a falling temperature. Schauberger referred to the resulting force as diamagnetic levitation power. He emphasised that nature already successfully used this direct, or 'reactionary', suction force, within weather generation, solar fusion stability etc.

Schauberger was given a team of scientists to help him with his work, and he insisted that these be treated not as prisoners but as free men - even though they were all technically prisoners of the Nazis. After their research headquarters were bombed, they were all transferred to Leonstein and there they perfected the "flying disc," powered by Schauberger's turbine which rotated air into a twisting type of oscillation resulting in a build-up of immense power causing levitation. Schauberger's prototype was developed into a vehicle that could speed 15000m in 3 minutes and fly in any direction at mach 3.

In what is now strangely reminiscent of current reports of alien spacecraft, the flying disc prototype, which rose and crashed against the laboratory ceiling, glowed blue-green as it rose, and left a silvery glow. Schauberger reportedly developed several prototypes of disc-shaped aircraft for the Nazis which worked on the following principles:

- MODEL I: The most conventional design, by today's concepts. It used a standard German Walther Rocket Engine and was steered by a conventional rudder.

- MODEL II: An improvement over Model I, with a radical departure, a specially designed rotary wing stabilized and steered the craft. This model was more maneuverable and faster.

EVIL AGENDA OF THE SECRET GOVERNMENT

■ MODEL III: Extremely fast, using a jet-vacuum (implosion) propulsion system capable of attaining speeds of over 6,000 kilometers per hour. The fuel mixture produced vapor trails, an acrid smell, and sometimes flames and sparks. The saucer's propulsion system produced high-pitched, whining sounds. The craft was capable of terrific acceleration or steady hover. It could climb and bank steeply and often startled the observer with loud sonic booms as it accelerated through the sound barrier. This model was equipped with telescopic landing gear.

Successors of MODEL III, still in the planning stage during the mid-1940's, utilized the Earth's magnetic field in their propulsion systems. Using the original implosion-powered propulsion system, these Nazi Saucers made no sound. They were flameless, odorless and smokeless. The outer skin of the hull, composed of a secret alloy called "impervium," pulsated eerily with various colors of the rainbow as the craft sped through the sky at velocities in excess of 10,000 kilometers per hour.

In a letter to a friend, Schauberger writes that he had worked at Matthausen concentration camp directing technically oriented prisoners and other German scientists in the successful construction of a saucer-shaped aircraft. In the letter, Schauberger gave further information from his direct experience with the German military.

"The flying saucer which was flight-tested on the 19th of February, 1945 near Prague and which attained a height of 15,000 meters in three minutes and a horizontal speed of 2,200 km/hours, was constructed according to a Mod 11 built at Mauthausen concentration camp in collaboration with the first-class engineers and stress-analysts assigned to me from the prisoners there. It was only after the end of the war that I came to hear through one of the workers under my direction, a Czech, that further intensive development was in progress. However, there was no further answer to my enquiry.

EVIL AGENDA OF THE SECRET GOVERNMENT

The amazing flying disk of the Germans as designed by
engineer Viktor Schauberger. To this day there is much in the way of
speculation as to where his ideas originated. Rumor has it that the
Nazi scientist had been involved in back engineering alien craft.

EVIL AGENDA OF THE SECRET GOVERNMENT

"From what I understand, just before the end of the war, the machine is supposed to have been destroyed on Keitel's orders. That's the last I heard of it. In this affair, several armament specialists were also involved who appeared at the works in Prague, shortly before my return to Vienna, and asked that I demonstrate the fundamental basis of it: The creation of an atomic low-pressure zone, which develops in seconds when either air or water is caused to move radially and axially under conditions of a falling temperature gradient."

Viktor Schauberger discovered that all nature operates with a dual principle, centripetence and centrifugence. Centripetence was called by Schauberger "Implosion or Impansion" to indicate a vortex action which condensed and cooled in the process. Experiments carried out by Schauberger included a levitating effect which could be achieved with the use of water or air.

At the end of the war, American military officers seized everything in the laboratory and, seeing Schauberger as a Nazi collaborator, put him into 'protective custody' for six months. The Munich publication, *Da Neue Zeitalter*, wrote in 1956 that "Viktor Schauberger was the inventor and discoverer of the new motive power, implosion, which, with the use of only air and water, generated light, heat and motion." The publication noted that the first unmanned flying disc was tested in 1945 near Prague, that it could hover motionless in the air and could fly as fast backwards as forwards. This flying disc was reported to have a diameter of 50 meters.

There is no doubt that Viktor Schauberger knew how to build a disc that levitated. However, he had not, at the time of his imprisonment, worked out how to "apply the brakes," as all his test flying discs eventually crashed.

After his imprisonment, Schauberger took up his research again. He had lost his financial assets but he still thought he could help the world by turning his inventive genius and insights to good use. He felt bitter about the effects of chemicals and

71

deforestation upon agriculture. He noted that: "the farmers work hand-in-hand with our foresters. The blood of the earth constantly weakens and the productivity of the soil decreases." When forests can no longer nurture water sources which supply vitality, farmlands downstream cannot build up voltage in the ground for keeping parasitic bacteria in balance, he observed. Noticing that the soil dried out after being ploughed with iron ploughs, he built copper plated ploughs. He continued to work on his agricultural ideas for some time.

In 1958 Schauberger, along with his son Walter, was asked to journey to the United States, where he was persuaded to provide a team of scientists, military and government officials with a record of everything he knew and to sign some contracts. However, he eventually became worried that his projects seemed to have been left sitting on the shelf, and that no further research was being done. He then discovered that in actual fact he had signed the rights to his work away to an industrial concern, and that this concern now retained power over the use and development of his work.

Concerned that his technology was being developed into new kinds of weapons systems, Schauberger fled the United States. On the afternoon of September 25th 1958, five days after arriving home, Viktor Schauberger died a broken man, reportedly crying that he had lost everything and that he no longer even owned himself.

NAZI UFOs: FACT OR FICTION?

Tim Matthews in his report: *Flying Saucers - Secret History*, writes: "We suspect that 'flying saucers' were developed, to some extent in parallel, on either side of the Atlantic during the Second World War. This realization, or understanding, is becoming increasingly a focus for research even though a long period of time has passed since those developments took place. Our research might be said to represent a 'small voice of calm' within the UFO community, whose increasingly shrill calls for Western governments to 'come clean about UFOs and aliens' tend to obscure the truth about flying saucers. To others, our research is an example of the 'Federal Hypothesis', that which states that: 'The answer seems to be that , in the USA at least, UFOs are controlled not so much by an intelligence as by an Intelligence Agency.'"

Despite the argument that German scientists had no more advanced technology than the allies, one American was very clear as to the technical achievements of Nazi scientists: Major General Hugh Knerr, Deputy Commanding General for Administration of US Strategic Forces in Europe, wrote to Lieutenant General Carl Spatz in March 1945: "Occupation of German scientific and industrial establishments has revealed the fact that we have been alarmingly backward in many fields of research, if we do not take this opportunity to seize the apparatus and the brains that developed it and put this combination back to work promptly, we will remain several years behind while we attempt to cover a field already exploited."

Even before the allies landed in Normandy in June 1944 special groups of language and technical research specialists had been organized in order to recover as much of the technological hardware and research data relating to advanced German weapons. This effort was dedicated to getting hold of much more than data on the V2 rocket, the most obvious and well-known example of German scientific expertise. Through an intelligence estimate passed to the allies via a Norwegian source and known as the "Oslo Letter," the allies were aware of other weapons under development and in operation by axis powers. These included radio-controlled bombs, huge guns, rocket launchers, new radar systems, long-range bombers and torpedoes. It would seem that they might also have been interested in a circular-wing aircraft with Vertical-Take-Off-and Landing (VTOL) capabilities.

One intelligence source indicates that from the mid 1930s there was significant interest in both Vertical-Take Off and-Landing (VTOL) and circular wing aircraft. This led to a number of designs one of which was the Focke-Wulf VTOL. Professor Heinrich Focke was particularly interested in emerging helicopter and autogyro technologies and was involved in the design and production of the **FW6, Fa223, Fa226, Fa283** and **284** models during the war. The creation of the jet engine encouraged him to design a propulsion system known as the "turbo-shaft" still used in most helicopters today.

In 1939 Focke patented a saucer-type aircraft with enclosed twin rotors. This was a revolutionary development described as follows:

"The exhaust nozzle forked in two at the end of the engine and ended in two auxiliary combustion chambers located on the trailing edge of the wing. When fuel was added to these combustion chambers they would act as afterburners to provide horizontal propulsion to Focke's design. The control at low speed was achieved by alternately varying the power from each auxiliary combustion chamber."

This was not the only circular aircraft under development at that time. Another similar aircraft was the troubled **AS6**, partly designed by the leading aviation expert in Germany Dr. Alexander Lippisch. Dr. Lippisch's work at the Gottingen Aviation Institute was extraordinary and his impact upon postwar 'UFOs' cannot be underestimated. His revolutionary "DM" series of small triangular aircraft were built and flown in conjunction with students at Darmstadt and Munich Universities and used rocket propulsion. The plans for these were transported to the USA after the war. His most advanced design was the Lippisch Supersonic Flying Wing. Although never built, the Lippisch Flying Wing resembles the triangle UFOs of the 1980s and 1990s.

Information about the **AS6** (V1) emerged in an article written by Hans Ebert and Hans Meier based upon information and a photograph provided by German aviation expert Wolfgang Spate. (Spate was the former Commander of Operational Test Unit 16 during the War and more recently recognized as a leading aviation expert. The article, entitled *Prototypen - Einselschicksale deutchser Flugzeuge, Der Kreisflugler AS6 V1*, was included in the respected Luftfahrt International in 1980.

EVIL AGENDA OF THE SECRET GOVERNMENT

The **AS6**, built by Messerschmidt, was based upon similar thinking as the Zimmerman **V173** "flying flapjack" - designed for use by the US Navy from 1942. The "flying flapjack" was far more successful and developed at the Chance-Vought works in Connecticut and despite its supposed limitations was a propeller-driven aircraft designed to be flown from an aircraft carrier, hence the need for Short Take off and Landing (STOL) capability. The flapjack was able to fly at low speeds of approximately 40mph. The flight envelope was 40-425 mph and a more advanced version, the **XF5U1**, was also tested.

One other important feature of these circular wings was an early stealth capability. The Horten brothers Reimar and Walter, known for their many successful flying wing prototypes, had developed a composite wing made of plywood held together by sawdust, charcoal and glue intended to absorb radar waves for use in their **HlX** model. This means that the circular wing or 'flying saucer' had a limited stealth capability years before the use of radar absorbent materials was considered for other advanced aircraft.

While it is likely that any information relating to the limited **AS6** would have been taken by the allies for examination at a later date it would seem that there is some evidence to suggest that a more advanced jet-powered flying saucer was at least designed, if not built, from around 1943 onwards.

SCHRIEVER'S FLYING TOP

Flight Captain Rudolph Schriever claimed in 1950 that he had worked with a small team at facilities near Prague with the goal to develop a flying saucer-type vehicle. The Schriever story first emerged in *Der Spiegel* magazine dated March 30th 1950 entitled *Untertassen-Flieger Kombination*:

EVIL AGENDA OF THE SECRET GOVERNMENT

"A former Luftwaffe captain and aircraft designer. Rudolph Schriever, who says engineers throughout the world experimented in the early 1940s with 'flying saucers' is willing to build one for the United States in six to nine months. The 40 year old Prague University graduate said he made blueprints for such a machine, which he calls a 'flying top,' before Germany's collapse and that the blueprints were stolen from his laboratory. He says the machine would be capable of 2,600 mph with a radius of 4,000 miles, Schriever is a US Army driver at Bremerhaven."

Schriever claimed that the model built for testing was completed in 1944 with a view to flying it in 1945. Nevertheless, the Russian advance ended any hopes of a test-flight. A 1975 Luftfahrt International report took these claims seriously and noted that after Schriever's death in the late 1950s papers found amongst his belongings had included technical drawings of a flying saucer.

Schriever seemed to argue that although a saucer had existed it had not flown. This is contradicted by a possible eyewitness, George Klein. Klein claimed in an interview, given on November 18th 1954 to the Zurich-based **Tages Anzeiger**, that he had actually seen a flying saucer test on 14th February 1945, and that the craft had performed remarkably well reaching an altitude of 30,000ft in 3 minutes as well as a high speed of hundreds of miles and hour. Despite the fact that subsequent information indicates that a jet-powered flying disc was developed at the end of the war Klein spoke of a "ray-guided disc." Despite this fanciful claim, some of the things he said sounded credible. For instance, Klein claimed that some of the work on the flying saucers had taken place at Pennemunde, the focal point for the development of the **A4/V2** rocket.

Klein also claimed that the necessary stability for the saucer had been attained through the use of a gyroscope. This is the same method used in the German rockets developed by the Von Braun/Dornberger team. It is claimed, by several other witnesses, that a flying saucer was tested in the vicinity of Kahla in Thuringia in early 1945. In 1946, the United States secretly brought over from Germany, one intact

EVIL AGENDA OF THE SECRET GOVERNMENT

Long before the CIA or other military groups, the Nazis had dug out huge complexes beneath the ground from which they conducted a variety of operations.

EVIL AGENDA OF THE SECRET GOVERNMENT

Kugelblitz which was taken to Wright- Patterson Air Base in Dayton, Ohio. There, the top secret aircraft was completely torn down and studied, piece by piece. When American scientists had finished, the Kugelblitz was then taken and quietly buried near the small village of Salem, Indiana.

SOVIET UFOs?

In 1954 the German magazine *Frankfurter Illustrierte*, ran a series of provocative articles claiming that flying saucers were developed and produced in the Soviet Union during World War II. The magazine gave detailed accounts of a top secret U. S. document that it said fully explained the flying saucer mystery.

In March 1944, a top secret file, number **250/eE**, was opened in Washington DC. The file told how an intelligence organization had dispatched 16 agents to a foreign country to conduct investigations of a highly classified nature.

In 1946 the agency removed the names of 14 agents, all lost on duty, but a fifteenth made it back to tell such an incredible story that officials passed it off as unbelievable. Another agent using the code name **PKR**, who had been listed as missing for three and a half years but during this time had been employed as a scientist's assistant in a Soviet laboratory, corroborated all that the first agent had reported and answered many questions the government had concerning flying saucers.

PKR told of a German scientist, Horst Pinkel, who in 1928 was involved in an exchange program of German and Russian officers. Pinkel, a high frequency expert, was the only officer who failed to return to his homeland a year later. According to **PKR**, Pinkel had been an ardent follower of a German doctor of engineering by the name of Walter Lewetzow. Lewetzow had developed some interesting theories on gravity and its interaction with light and energy that had received some ridicule from the German scientific community.

Pinkel had advanced Lewetzow's theory into the following form -- that the entire universe is filled with rays whose particles or waves, traveling in all directions, cause a neutral and balancing effect on all matter. Pinkel believed that if these rays were harnessed and controlled, they could be the source of a power almost equaling that needed to create what most scientists referred to as "the impossible perpetual motion." Pinkel claimed that if one ever succeeded in weakening and controlling the rays, the world would have a colossal, practical and everlasting source of energy.

PKR reported that Horst Pinkel had first taken over a huge building at the edge of the town of Kaluga near Moscow in 1930 and, with all necessary materials available to him, proceeded to research the theoretical rays. By 1938, he had successfully proven his theory through experiment and observation. Three years later, he had finished developing instrumentation for measuring the strange new rays.

PKR said that a special laboratory in Magnitogorsk was the next place where Pinkel was moved. In this laboratory, he discovered that the rays belonged to a new category whose single rays change with a terrific speed from the character of ordinary waves into the clear character of corpuscles. He found that "the rhythm of change of the oscillation-frequency remained parallel," stated **PKR**'s report.

In November 1942, Pinkel, with a group of Russian scientists and inventors, moved to the district of Belaja in the south Urals where a secret MVD-supervised laboratory was set up. The Kremlin had hoped that Pinkel could finish the project in time to construct a powerful new weapon for use against the Germans, but time ran out. PKR was able to bring back to the US the exact formula for an alloy which Pinkel had developed for use in fabricating a craft utilizing the powerful new rays.

EVIL AGENDA OF THE SECRET GOVERNMENT

Air Marshal Konstantin Wershinin took over the Installations of Science in May 1948 and urged his scientists to complete more of the craft, which had terrific speeds and a potential sphere of action the same as the "radius of the universe." At that time, **PKR** reported, five flying saucers had been constructed in the Soviet Union. **PKR** also brought back plans for construction of such a craft and the precise data for harnessing the fantastic ray that Pinkel had discovered.

.

In May 1949, the soviet newspaper Pravda surprised many observers by quoting one of Russia's most famous aeronautical engineers: "If ever an aircraft from earth lands on one of the heavenly bodies, it will be Soviet." Pravda has long been considered the Soviet Union's foremost propaganda outlet.

The *Frankfurter Illustrierte* concluded its series by reporting that in February 1952, an announcement from the Soviet Zialkowski Laboratory claimed the Russians were at work on a "Space Island" that would allow a stop-over for space vehicles flying from earth to "other particles in the Universe."

NAZI SPACECRAFT

Vladimir Terziski is a Bulgarian born engineer and physicist, who graduated Cum Laude from the Master of Science program of Tokai University in Tokyo in 1980. He served as a solar energy researcher at the Bulgarian Academy of Sciences before immigrating to the U.S. in 1984.

Terziski believes that some UFO sightings could be spacecraft from other planets. However, Terziski thinks that there are also craft constructed by the Bavarian Illuminati (the Secret Group) which are taking advantage of the alien question by attempting to pass off their own black projects as alien technology. Although Terziski is uncertain as to the existence of the so-called Greys, he does admit his belief in an ancient human-like society which possesses antigravity craft. Terziski states that whether or not extraterrestrials exist, the New World Order may be using the alien threat as a means to bring about world unity after the fall of Russia while "at the same time hundreds of valid, but undesirable ET contacts with more advanced races are debunked or ignored by the government."

Terziski alleges that the Secret Group has been involved in top secret space Research and Development since the turn of the century, and that the Nazis, the American Eastern Establishment, and the KGB has been involved as well. In other words, the lower classes of all these nations were themselves largely unfamiliar with such top secret research, although the Nazis working in the highest levels of internationalism were and are intricately involved in the situation.

Although it may sound incredible, Terziski alleges that he possesses information such as the first video expose of Nazi UFOs. German/Japanese saucer landings on the moon and Mars in 1944-46, Marconi group's landing on Mars in 1956, video footage of Nazi interplanetary dreadnoughts, and a secret Soviet-American saucer landing on Mars in the 1960's.

The Germans allegedly landed on the moon as early as 1942, utilizing their larger exo-atmospheric rocket saucers of the Miethe and Schriever type. The Miethe rocket craft was built in diameters of 15 and 50 meters, and the Schriever Walter turbine powered craft was designed as an interplanetary exploration vehicle. It had a diameter of 60 meters, had 10 floors of crew compartments, and stood 45 meters high.

Since their first day of landing on the moon, the Germans started boring and tunneling under the surface, and by the end of the war there was a small Nazi research base on the moon. The free energy tachyon drive craft of the Haunibu-1 and 2 type were used after 1944 to haul people, material and the first robots to the construction site on the moon. When Russians and Americans secretly landed together on the moon in the early fifties with their own saucers, they spent their first night there as guests of the Nazis in their underground base. In the sixties a massive Russian - American base had been built on the moon, that now has a population of 40,000 people.

According to the authors of an underground German documentary from the Thule Society, the only constructed craft of the Haunibu - 3 type, the 74 meter diameter naval warfare dreadnought, was chosen for a trip to Mars. The Haunibu - 3 was saucer shaped, had the bigger Andromeda tachyon drives, and was armed with four triple gun turrets of large naval caliber (three inverted upside down and attached to the underside of the craft, and the fourth on top of the crew compartments).

A volunteer suicide crew of Germans and Japanese was chosen, because everybody knew that this journey was a one-way trip with no return. The large intensity of the electro-gravitic fields and the inferior quality of the metal alloys used then for the structural elements of the drive, was causing the metal to fatigue and get very brittle after only few months of work. The flight to Mars departed from Germany one month before the war ended in April 1945.

The ship contained a large crew, numbering in the hundreds because of the low level of automation and electronic controls inside the saucer. Most of the systems of the craft had to be operated like those on a U-boat of that time, manually. Because the structurally weakened tachyon drives were not working with full power, the trip to Mars took almost eight months to accomplish.

An initial trust towards Mars was probably accomplished using the strong gravitational field of Earth, after that the craft coasted for eight months in an elliptical orbit to Mars with its main drives turned off. Later trips to Mars by the joint Soviet - U.S. craft in 1952 reached Mars in only 2 - 3 days, because their drives were working during the whole flight, accelerating in the first half and decelerating in the second.

EVIL AGENDA OF THE SECRET GOVERNMENT

Is it possible that with the help of Nazi
scientists that the secret government
landed on Mars decades ago...establishing
bases ahead of NASA?

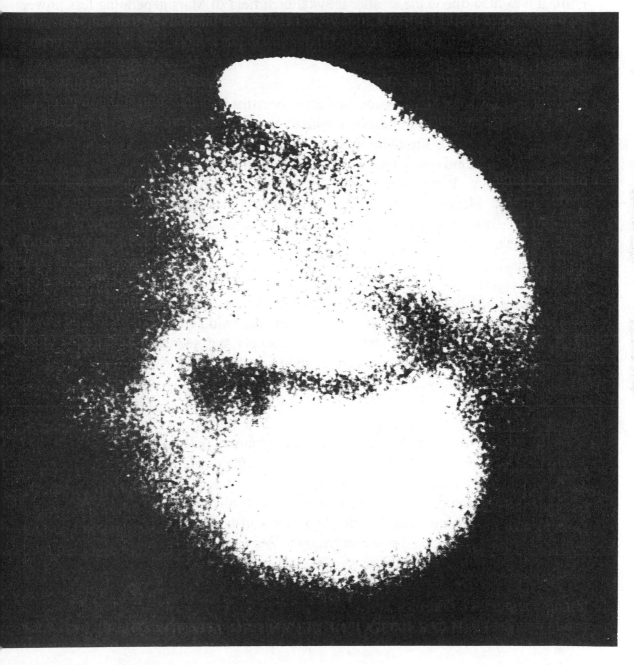

EVIL AGENDA OF THE SECRET GOVERNMENT

After a disastrous, almost crash landing, the saucer slammed to a stop, damaging irreparably its engines, but saving the crew. That happened in the middle of January 1946. The crash landing on Mars was not only due to the crippled tachyon drives of the craft, it was also due to the smaller gravitational field of Mars generating less power for the tachyon drives; and also due to the thinner atmosphere on Mars, that could not be used as effectively for air breaking as the Earth's atmosphere could.

The craft was shaped as a giant saucer, a form that is very efficient as an air brake, when it is entered into the atmosphere with its huge cross section perpendicular to the trajectory of descent. The radio message with the mixed news was received by the German underground space control center in Neuschwabenland, and by their research base on the moon. It is not known what happened to the crew of the ill-fated Haunibu - 3 spacecraft. However, if the story is true, their bodies probably still remain on the cold lonely surface of the red planet, waiting to be discovered and brought back to mother Earth.

On a June 5, 1993 interview with talk-show host Sam Russellon on K-TALK radio in Salt Lake City, Utah. Vladimir Terziski made the bold assertion that in one way or another, any independent scientist who discovers the secret of electromagnetic "free-energy" antigravity - propulsion, is soon bought off, black-listed or killed by the Bavarian Illuminati.

The Secret Group has for centuries been extremely determined to maintain their monopoly on such technology and keep it out of the hands of the masses. The military arm of the Bavarian Empire, the Third Reich, was allowed to field test much of this technology under supervision during World War II as the Bavarians were intent on establishing the "New World Order," by force if necessary. The defeat of Nazi Germany however, forced the Secret Group to flee Europe to their already established secret base located in Antarctica.

Chapter Six

SECRET PROJECTS IN ANTARTICA, POLAR OPENINGS AND ANTIGRAVITY DISCS

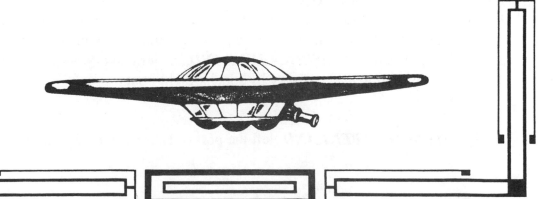

EVIL AGENDA OF THE SECRET GOVERNMENT

The historical beginnings of German interest and research into the Antarctic or South Polar region began in 1873 when Sir Edward Dallman on behalf of the newly founded German Society of Polar Research discovered new Antarctic routes with his ship *GRONLAND*. Dallman discovered the "Kaiser-Wilhelm-Inseln" at the western entrance of the Biskmarkstrasse along the Biscoue Islands.

Exploring the polar regions, the Germans were already quite innovative, for the *GRONLAND* was the first steamship to see the Antarctic ice. Within the next 60 years 2 further expeditional thrusts took place, and two complete expeditions were fulfilled, namely 1910 under Wilhem Filchner with his ship *DEUTSCHLAND*, and 1925 with the special designed polar expedition ship, the *METEOR* under the command of Dr. Albert Merz.

During the years before WWII the Germans claim to parts of Antarctica and the wish to possess their own base there grew stronger. By this time proof of Germany's claim to Antarctica by employing a single military strike seemed to be the best option. Hitler himself was anxious for a foothold in the Antarctic and such a claim could be used for National Socialistic propaganda and a further demonstration of the new "Superpower Germany."

On the other hand, for political reasons, provoking the Allies had to be avoided. Germany was at this time not completely prepared for the coming war. As a matter of fact, the idea of a semi-civilian expedition in cooperation with the German national airline company, the **LUFTHANSA** developed. The command on this strike was given to the polar-experienced Captain Alfred Ritscher, who had already led some expeditions to the North Pole and proved courage and skill in critical situations. The selected ship was the *MS SCHWABENLAND*, a German aircraft carrier used since 1934 for transatlantic mail delivery by special flight-boats.

The *MS SCHWABENLAND* left the port of Hamburg on December 17th 1938 heading to the Antarctic on a precisely planned and determined route that reached the ice on January 19th 1939. The following weeks on 15 flights the flight-boats *PASSAT* and the *BOREAS* flew across some 600.000 square kilometers and made more than 11.000 pictures of the area. Nearly one fifth of the whole Antarctic area was scanned this way, thus documented for the first time and simultaneous claimed to be German territory. To stress this claim on the outside too, the two planes dismissed several thousands of drop-flags, special metal poles with expedition's insignia on them, the "swastika." The whole territory was renamed NEUSCHWABENLAND.

In 1938, long before the end of the Second World War, the Nazis continued to send out numerous exploratory missions to the Queen Maud region of Antarctica. A steady stream of expeditions were reportedly sent out from South Africa. Over 230,000 square miles of the frozen continent were mapped from the air, and the Germans discovered vast regions that were surprisingly free of ice, as well as warm water lakes and cave inlets.

One vast ice cave within the glacier was reportedly found to extend 30 miles to a large hot-water geothermal lake deep below. Various scientific teams were moved in to the area, including hunters, trappers, collectors and zoologists, botanists, agriculturists, plant specialists, mycologists, parasitologist, marine biologists, ornithologists, and many others. Numerous divisions of the German government were involved in the top secret project.

After all the data was gathered, deep underground construction teams came pouring into the area. They came on cargo ships, military transport ships, and submarines. The cargo ships coming from South Africa were protected by a host of killer-submarines and military ships. This might explain the intense Nazi war efforts in North and South Africa. Any ship that even came close to the shipping routes from South Africa to Antarctica were destroyed by German U-boats to protect the secret.

EVIL AGENDA OF THE SECRET GOVERNMENT

After all the goods were brought, the VIPs and scientists started to show up with a compliment of ULTRA, a highly specialized Nazi SS team. The construction and secret projects in Antarctica continued throughout the entire course of the war. Just before the end of WWII, two German provision U-boats, U-530 and U-977, were launched from a port on the Baltic Sea. Reportedly they took with them members of the antigravity-disc research and development teams, and the last of the most vital flying disc components. This included the notes and drawings for the latest saucer or aerial disc designs, and designs for the gigantic underground complexes and living accommodations based on the remarkable underground factories of Nordhausen in the Harz Mountains.

The two U-boats reached the new land of Neuschwabenland where they unloaded their secret cargo. On July 10, 1945, more than two months after the end of the War, the German submarine U-530 surrendered to Argentine authorities. The Commander was Otto Wermoutt. The sub had a crew of 54 men (the normal sub crew was 18 men) and the cargo consisted of 540 barrels of cigarettes and unusually large stocks of food. The Commander was 25 years old, the second officer was 22, and the crew was an average of 25 except for one man who was 32 years old. This was an unusually young crew and upon questioning it was learned that they all claimed that they had no relatives.

The crew of the U-Boat were interrogated by U.S. Intelligence agents who had suspected the existence of the Antarctic base. Whatever the Nazi soldiers tried to tell them, apparently the Americans were not convinced. The Antarctican's were desperate following the war, and knew that a confrontation was imminent. Much effort was put into developing secret weapons projects to defend their new underground Empire, which no doubt was constructed with the help of a large number of expendable slave laborers transported from the concentration camps of Europe. The major base-city of Antarctica became known as the New Berlin, or by the code-name "Base-211."

EVIL AGENDA OF THE SECRET GOVERNMENT

Does this map show the location of the ice free city that is said to
exist within a glacier at the South Pole that has been
given the code name "New Berlin" or "Base 211?"

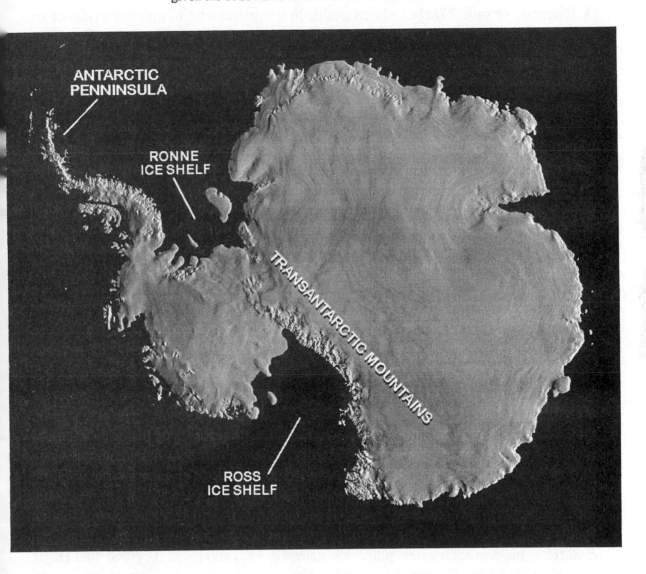

EVIL AGENDA OF THE SECRET GOVERNMENT

HITLER: DEAD OR ALIVE?

Starting in the early 1950s, rumors that Hitler had escaped to a secret Nazi base at the South Pole began to circulate in the press and by world of mouth. In 1952, Dwight D. Eisenhower said: "We have been unable to unearth one bit of tangible evidence of Hitler's death. Many people believe that Hitler escaped from Berlin." When President Truman asked Joseph Stalin at the Potsdam conference in 1945 whether or not Hitler was dead, Stalin replied bluntly, "No." Stalin's top army officer, Marshall Gregory Zhukov, whose troops were the ones to occupy Berlin, stated after a long thorough investigation in 1945, "We have found no corpse that could be Hitler's."

The chief of the U.S. trial counsel at Nuremberg, Thomas J. Dodd, said, "No one can say Hitler is dead." Major General Floyd Parks, who was commanding general of the U.S. sector in Berlin, stated for publication that he had been present when Marshall Zhukov described his entrance to Berlin, and Zhukov stated he believed Hitler might have escaped. Lt. Gen. Bedell Smith, Chief of Staff to Gen. Eisenhower in the European invasion and later Director of the CIA, stated publicly on Oct. 12, 1945, "No human being can say conclusively that Hitler is dead."

Col. W.J. Heimlich, former Chief, United States Intelligence, at Berlin, stated that he was in charge of determining what had happened to Hitler and after a thorough investigation his report was, "There was no evidence beyond that of hearsay to support the theory of Hitler's suicide." He also stated, "On the basis of present evidence, no insurance company in America would pay a claim on Adolph Hitler."

Nuremberg judge Michael Mussmanno said in his book *Ten Days to Die*, that "Russia must accept much of the blame that Hitler did not die in May 1945." However, Mussmanno stated that he interviewed Hitler's personal waiter, his valet, his chauffeur, his two secretaries, pilots, top generals, etc., and they all agreed that Hitler committed suicide. He said they could not have gotten together afterward and made up a story that agreed in perfect detail without one flaw anywhere, so they must be telling the truth and he was absolutely convinced that Hitler committed suicide.

Former Secretary of State Jimmy Byrnes in his book *Frankly Speaking*, states: "While in Potsdam at the Conference of the Big Four, Stalin left his chair, came over and clinked his liquor glass with mine in a very friendly manner. I said to him: 'Marshal Stalin, what is your theory about the death of Hitler?' Stalin replied: "He is not dead. He escaped either to Spain or Argentina.'"

The September, 1948, issue of a magazine called *The Plain Truth* carried a headline article: *IS HITLER ALIVE, OR DEAD?*, subtitled: "Here is summarized the conclusions of an exhaustive three-year investigation -- together with reasons for believing Hitler may be alive and secretly planning the biggest hoax of all history." Another article in November, 1949, says "The Nazis went underground, May 16, 1943!" and details a meeting at the residence of Krupp von Bohlen-Halbach, the head of I.G. FARBEN, etc., at which they planned "for World War III."

An article published in August, 1952, entitled *HITLER DID NOT DIE*, was subtitled "Adolph Hitler's fake suicide in his Berlin Bunker now is exposed as History's greatest hoax! Positive evidence comes to light that Hitler did not die -- here's new evidence that Hitler is alive, directing the Nazi underground, today!" The June, 1952, issue of "The Plain Truth" is headlined: "Hitler May Be Alive!" The article states:

"Now, new facts, or purported facts, leak out. It's reported now that in 1940 the Nazis started to amass tractors, planes, sledges, gliders, and all sorts of machinery and materials in the South polar regions that for the next 4 years Nazi technicians built, on an almost unknown continent, Antarctica, the Fuhrer's Shangrala, a new Berchtesgaden." The report says: "They scooped out an entire mountain, built a new refuge completely camouflaged a magic mountain hide-a-way. The recently discovered continent is larger than Europe, 5,600 miles from Africa, 1,900 miles from

EVIL AGENDA OF THE SECRET GOVERNMENT

Hitler leads a personally selected
group of SS officials and others who
followed his doctrine closely.

the southern tip of South America, 4,800 miles from Australia. It is not a mere ice-covered surface, but a real continent, with plains, valleys, mountain peaks up to 15,000 feet. The temperature in the interior is around zero in the summer, and never drops below 20 or 30 degrees below in the winter. In other words, it is not as cold as in parts of North Dakota or Canada."

Bonjour magazine, the *Police Gazette*, and the Paris newspaper *Le Monde*, all had articles about Hitler's South Pole hideaway. Admiral Doenitz, in 1943, stated, "The German submarine fleet has even now established an earthly paradise, an impregnable fortress, for the Fuhrer, in whatever part of the world." Although he did not specify where the exact location was, *Bonjour* pointed out that in 1940 Nazi engineers had begun construction of buildings that were to withstand temperatures to 60 degrees below zero. In 1981, Donald McKale wrote *Hitler: The Survival Myth*, to try to lay to rest the questions about what happened to Hitler. The introduction says: "In this book a distinguished historian examines the postwar world's most absorbing and persistent mystery, revealing why it has endured and where the mystery leads."

Recent TV documentaries are still proclaiming, "at last, the final, once and for all, this is the real story" about what happened to Hitler, yet they all do not really answer the question. One program, called "*What Really Happened to Adolph Hitler*," after investigating numerous stories, ends by saying that, in spite of Glasnost and the new freedom of access to Russian files, the files on Hitler are still some of the most highly classified items of the Soviets.

The Diario Illustrado of Santiago, Chile, January 18, 1948 issue, reported: "On 30th of April, 1945, Berlin was in dissolution but little of that dissolution was evident at Templehof Airfield. At 4:15 PM a JU52 landed and S.S. troops directly from Rechlin for the defense of Berlin disembarked, all of them young, not older than 18 years." The writer said, "The gunner in the particular plane was an engineer whom I had known for a number of years and for whom I had endeavored to get exemption from military service. He sought to tank up and leave Berlin as quickly as possible.

EVIL AGENDA OF THE SECRET GOVERNMENT

"During this re-fueling interval he was suddenly elbowed in the ribs by his radio operator with a nod to look in a certain direction. At about 100-120 meters he saw a sleek ARADO 234, he and the radio operator saw, without any doubt whatsoever, standing in front of the jet, their Commander in Chief, Adolf Hitler, dressed in field-grey uniform and gesticulating animatedly with some Party functionaries, who were obviously seeing him off. For about ten minutes whilst their plane was being refueled the two men observed this scene and around 4:30 PM they took to the air again. They were extremely astonished to hear during the midnight military news bulletin, some seven and a half hours later, that Hitler had committed suicide."

On a Canadian Broadcasting Corporation program called "As It Happens," September 17th, 1974 at 7:15 PM, a Prof. Dr. Ryder Saguenay, oral surgeon from the Dental Faculty of the University of California at Los Angeles, said that Hitler had ordered a special plane to leave from Berlin with all medical and dental records, especially X-rays, of all top Nazis for an unknown destination. He said that the dental records used to identify Hitler's body were drawn from memory by a dental assistant, who later disappeared and was never found.

An editorial in *Zig Zag*, Santiago, Chile, January 16, 1948, states that on April 30th, 1945, Flight Captain Peter Baumgart took Adolf Hitler, his wife Eva Braun, as well as a few loyal friends by plane from Tempelhof Airport to Tondern in Denmark. From Tondern, they took another plane to Kristiansund in Norway. From there they joined a submarine convoy.

The writer Michael Bar-Zohar in *The Avengers*, p. 99, said: "In 1943 Admiral Doenitz had declared: 'The German U-boat fleet is proud to have made an earthly paradise, an impregnable fortress for the Fuhrer, somewhere in the world.' He did not say in what part of the world it existed, but fairly obviously it was in South America."

The German writer Ernst Zundel under the pseudonym "Mattern Friedrich" reported

EVIL AGENDA OF THE SECRET GOVERNMENT

"America didn't win the war. Hitler won World War II."
Guatemalan president Jose Arevalo, 1951

that Admiral Doenitz told a 1944 graduating class of naval cadets in Kiel: "The German Navy has still a great role to play in the future. The German Navy knows all hiding places for the Navy to take the Fuhrer to, should the need arise. There he can prepare his last measures in complete quiet."

The newspaper *France Soir* had the following account: "Almost 1-1/2 years after cessation of hostilities in Europe, the Icelandic whaler, **Juliana** was stopped by a large German U-boat. The **Juliana** was in the Antarctic region around the Malvinas (now Falkland) Islands when a German submarine surfaced and raised the German official naval Flag of Mourning, red with a black edge. The submarine commander sent out a boarding party, which approached the **Juliana** in a rubber dinghy, and having boarded the whaler demanded of Capt. Hekla part of his fresh food stocks. The request was made in the definite tone of an order to which resistance would have been unwise. The German officer spoke a correct English and paid for his provisions in U.S. dollars, giving the Captain a bonus of $10 for each member of the **Juliana** crew. While the food stuffs were being transferred to the submarine, the submarine commander informed Capt. Hekla of the exact location of a large school of whales. Later the **Juliana** found the school of whales where designated."

ADMIRAL BYRD'S SECRET WAR IN ANTARCTICA

By 1946 the secret Antarctic base, New Berlin, was beginning to make its presence known through incursions into the airspaces of the United States and Soviet Union. These incursions were being made with the Nazis high technology flying discs. New, improved versions of the Kugelblitz were now able to fly at super-sonic speeds, and reach most major cities on the planet. The Nazis message to their old enemies was clear, "we can fly in your airspace with impunity, there is nothing you can do to stop us."

EVIL AGENDA OF THE SECRET GOVERNMENT

In December 1947, Admiral Richard E. Byrd led 4,000 military troops from the U.S., Britain and Australia in an invasion of Antarctica. Called Operation Highjump, the mission consisted of three battle groups from Norfolk, VA. They were led by Byrd's command ship, the ice-breaker **Northwind**, and consisted of the catapult ship **Pine Island**, the destroyer **Brownsen**, the aircraft-carrier **Philippines Sea**, the U.S. submarine **Sennet**, two support vessels, **Yankee** and **Merrick**, two tankers **Canisted** and **Capacan**, the destroyer **Henderson** and a floatplane ship **Currituck**.

On March 5, 1947 the *El Mercurio* newspaper of Santiago, Chile, ran the article "On Board the Mount Olympus on the High Seas" which quoted Byrd in an interview by Lee van Atta: "Adm. Byrd declared today that it was imperative for the United States to initiate immediate defense measures against hostile regions. The admiral further stated that he didn't want to frighten anyone unduly but that it was a bitter reality that in case of a new war the continental United States would be attacked by flying objects which could fly from pole to pole at incredible speeds." Admiral Byrd repeated the same points of view, resulting from his personal knowledge gathered both at the north and south poles, before a news conference held for the International News Service."

The only official statement on the purpose of the task force related the need for testing "new material under the extreme Antarctic conditions." The force started up at the established US bases in the Ross Sea, then it moved up the western Antarctic coast heading toward the Northern Antarctic coast and Nueschwabenland, building up a bridgehead on January 27th 1947 somewhere west of it. The operation was planned and equipped for a full 6-8 month duration, but had pulled out by February, 1947. Officially the expedition was declared a big success because it delivers many new facts of the use of military equipment under extreme conditions.

Although the entire expedition lasted some 8 weeks, some sources claim that the actual battle, once Byrd's forces had been divided into three main battle groups on the continent of Antarctica, lasted only 3 weeks after encountering heavy resistance from

EVIL AGENDA OF THE SECRET GOVERNMENT

Nazi flying discs. One thing that Admiral Byrd stated in a press conference after his defeat at Antarctica was that the Antarctic continent should be surrounded by a "wall of defense installations since it represented the last line of defense for America."

When Byrd returned to the States, he was hospitalized and was not allowed to hold any more press conferences. It was reported that Admiral Byrd went into a rage before the President and Joint Chiefs of Staff and in an almost demanding tone, strongly "suggested" that Antarctica be turned into a thermonuclear test range. The United States response was to pull out of Antarctica for almost ten years.

In March 1955, Byrd was placed in charge of Operation Deepfreeze which was part of the International Geophysical Year (1957-1958) exploration of the Antarctic. Both the Soviets and the United States have ringed the poles with defense and detection bases, and in between was the barren no-man's-land of the poles where absolutely nobody lived, or did they? Could it be that we pretended we were protecting against the Russians and they pretended they were protecting against us, while really we and they were both scared of what was in between us, the Nazi Last Battalion?

Since that time, there have been rumors about Germans counterfeiting U.S. currency and obtaining American money printing plates, which may account for the German use of American money. The Nazis, from their Antarctic base, which is reported to be the real power behind the New World Order, began to slowly infiltrate into Argentina, Chile, and up into the United States.

The Secret Group bought large tracts of land and swept up corporations. They also invested in corporations in Germany and elsewhere, with plans to make a comeback. They used the German treasury, captured treasure from other nations, and counterfeit American currency printed on real United States currency printing plates given to the Russians and captured by the Germans. The Nazi elite has started to accomplish via stealth what they failed to do by force in World Wars I and II, by infiltrating North and

EVIL AGENDA OF THE SECRET GOVERNMENT

South America and engaging in economic warfare from their extensive underground "black budget" empire below Antarctica and also South and North America, with the help of their allies in the CIA/NSA.

The late 40s and 50s were spent putting their agents in place and rebuilding their main clients European industrial base, with American money. At the end of World War II, Nelson Rockefeller reportedly brought 3000 high Nazi party officials from Germany illegally into the United States. As of today it is believed that there are now 1.6 million Nazis in the United States, many in high level government and major corporations. Incredibly, these Nazis are attempting to set up a "Forth Reich" to continue the thousand-year plan of Adolph Hitler, with its intent to eventually eliminate all "non Aryan" people, dissidents and undesirables.

The initial steps in the American overthrow occurred in the 1960's through several of the Group's most critical agents, Earl Warren and LBJ, with assists from J. Edgar Hoover and others. Supposedly, Chief Justice Warren, unlike LBJ, was an unwilling agent. The Group forced Warren to participate in the JFK cover-up and the Group's plan to alter the social structure of US because they "had something on him." One of the first things the Group did to protect its own covert operation was one of Reinhard Gehlen's specialties in WWII Nazi intelligence, divert attention to the "Red menace."

Chapter Seven

MIND CONTROL, BRAINWASHING, GENETIC EXPERIMENTS & GLOBAL KIDNAPPINGS

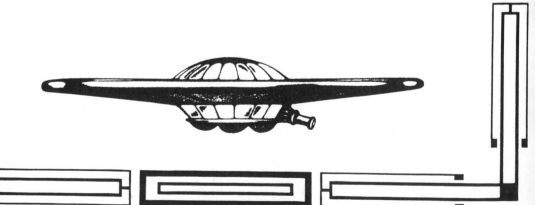

EVIL AGENDA OF THE SECRET GOVERNMENT

The Antarctic base, New Berlin, has also been home to Nazi experiments in mind control, genetics, and hybridization (between humans and animals), which were apparently aided by the discovery and perfection of the Tesla scaler-wave microscope which helped the Secret Group to unlock the human genome. By the end of the 1980's, New Berlin reportedly contained a population of over 2,000,000 people loyal to the Nazi philosophy. These include so-called pure-bred "Aryan SS" who apparently utilize slave labor to expand their underground empire.

The slave labor used by the Secret Group is obtained by worldwide "kidnaping rings." These rings usually take homeless children from poverty stricken countries, and disturbingly enough, children from the United States, Canada and Europe. Nazi doctors have developed a certain drug that could be used on children inducing severe pain and torture, where the child would normally black out, and become unconscious. The doctor could administer the drug and it would keep the child from blacking out, and thus the doctor could then inflict greater pain, going far beyond the threshold of human endurance, which in turn would allow the mind of the child to become totally wiped out, creating a new slave.

The children would need to be totally programmed from the beginning, starting from a blank consciousness. This technique of brainwashing or mind control allowed them to create whatever kind of person they wanted. The Nazis created many of these children to become sex slaves. The children were then used by others for as long as they were needed, only to be disposed of when they were no longer useful.

Joseph Mengele, the Nazi doctor that worked closely with Adolf Hitler, did not die at the end of the war as reports have indicated. Dr. Mengele, thanks to Operation Paperclip, was secretly brought into the United States where he set up a mind control research center in Florida, which specialized in manipulating the minds of children. The research conducted by Mengele was later developed and used by several United States intelligence agencies to build up a cache of unwitting "moles," ready to serve as assassins or spies when the need arose.

EVIL AGENDA OF THE SECRET GOVERNMENT

Hitler was a big believer in the existence of a world within our globe which he said was populated by a super race of beings whom he hoped would help him establish the New World Order.

EVIL AGENDA OF THE SECRET GOVERNMENT

The idea of dealing with children fascinated the Nazis because their minds were already easily controlled and easier to alter than those of adults. Plus, they had the ability to control them with greater ease because of size, and also they had the ability to use a mind-controlled child according to the way they wished. Dr. Mengele's continued experiments in Mind control has led to today's technological advancements in the field of electronic mind control and behavioral modification.

Most of today's knowledge of human mind control can be directly traced back to Nazi research during and after the war. This research was eagerly sought by the United States which later used this information to conduct further research such as the CIA Project MKULTRA (1953-62), which explored the possibilities of hypnosis, conditioning, sensory deprivation, drugs, religious cults, microwaves, psychosurgery, brain implants, ESP, and psychoelectronics.

"Former" Nazi scientists and doctors under the authority of the CIA and NSA found that their experiments on unwitting human subjects presented the problem of "disposal," pushing them out of windows or locking them away in mental institutions could lead to awkward questions. A solution could be found in erasing the memories of the victims, with the added bonus of being useful in a clandestine context, as an ex CIA employee by the name of Victor Marchetti explains: "Amnesia was a big goal, the agent doesn't even know what he's done, you send him in, he does the job. When he comes out, you clean him out."

The problem with hypnotically induced amnesia is "leakage," dreams or flashbacks of the repressed material. The installation of a "screen memory" would ensure that any recollection would be of a false memory. Dr Orne (CIA scientist and board member of the False Memory Syndrome Foundation) writes, " this phenomenon is easier to produce than total amnesia, perhaps because it eliminates the subjective feeling of an empty space in memory." Extra layers of confusion can be added by hypnotically creating multiple personalities, providing an array of cover stories.

EVIL AGENDA OF THE SECRET GOVERNMENT

Alleged UFO abductees who recollect being experimented on by the Greys may be experiencing "screen" memories of CIA surgical and psychological testing. Abductees often report surgical procedures being conducted on them. They recall having needles inserted in their brains or objects inserted up their nose. Implants are alleged to have been found by X-Rays and MRI scans of abductees brains. These objects could be of terrestrial origin, a device called the "stimociever" was invented in the 50's by Jose Delgado, author of *Physical Control of the Mind* : *Toward a Psychocivilized Society*.

Delgado was a CIA funded researcher into methods of electronic stimulation of the brain. The stimociever is a miniature electrode placed within the brain which can receive and transmit electronic signals over FM radio waves. Delgado claimed that "motion, emotion and behavior can be directed by physical forces and that humans can be controlled like robots by push buttons." His research showed that electronic stimulation of the brain via the stimociever could create a variety of effects including "colored visions" and "floating" sensations, familiar features of abduction accounts.

Alleged alien abduction stories are not the only source of supposed implant occurrences. "Wavies," the victims of non-ionizing radiation (microwave) research are recounting tales of having been implanted. Robert Naeslund claims to have been implanted in the 60's by the Swedish Secret Police (SAPO) in conjunction with the CIA. He has X-Ray "evidence" and has had the device removed by a sympathetic doctor. He first realized that something had happened to him when he suffered an inexplicable nosebleed, a regular occurrence in alien abductions.

A 1977 scientific paper, *Quantization of Microwave Biological Effects,* describes the use of nasally implanted electrodes in animals to measure the effects of electromagnetic radiation. A Finnish "wavie," Martti Koski, claims to have been experimented on while visiting Canada. During the course of one session he was told that the doctors tampering with him were "aliens from Sirius." Another time he was told that he was under the direction of "the Lord." The book, *Abductions* by Jenny Randles, details a 1965 incident where a woman claimed that her husband allowed her to be abducted and physically examined. During the process, one of the abductors laughed and remarked "They will think it's flying saucers." If not flying saucers, then what? And why?

In 1967, Lincoln Lawrence wrote a JFK assassination book, *Were We Controlled?* which asserted Oswald was a hypnoprogrammed assassin with a malfunctioning implant in his brain. Lawrence was the first to reveal the method of RHIC-EDOM (Radio-Hypnotic Intracerebral Control / Electronic Dissolution Of Memory), which apparently can turn men into electronically controlled robots programmed to kill on command.

RHIC consists of conditioning the victim to enter a deep trance at the sound of a specific tone transmitted to a brain implant, "Under RHIC, a 'sleeper' can be used years later with no realization that the 'sleeper' is even being controlled. He can be made to perform acts that he will have no memories of having ever carried out...nothing he says will implicate the group or government which possessed and controlled him."

The second stage of the process, Electronic Dissolution of Memory, involves the electronic interference of neurotransmitters to create amnesia, "There is already in use a small EDOM generator- transmitter which can be concealed on the body of a person. Contact with the person, a casual handshake or even just a touch, transmits a tiny electronic charge plus an ultrasonic signal tone which for a short while will disturb the time orientation of the person affected."

In 1975, journalist James L. Moore claimed that he had been given information on RHIC-EDOM by two CIA agents which detailed how the method could be put to use. "A person may be placed under control without his knowledge, programmed to perform certain actions and maintain certain attitudes, effective for a lifetime, control maybe triggered months or even years after the first hypnosis and programming. The emotion of anger can be created by artificial radio signals sent to your brain."

EVIL AGENDA OF THE SECRET GOVERNMENT

` If RHIC-EDOM exists it could explain abductee symptoms such as implants, missing time, personality shifts and repeat abductions. However, even if it doesn't, there are still other methods of interfering with the human mind. Recent years have seen a proliferation of "mind machines" providing drugless highs. One device is the Hemisync, a slightly different frequency played into each ear results in the brain calculating the difference between the two producing a binaural beat in which the brain then entrains itself. The brain can be entrained to produce Alpha and Beta waves which make the subject open to suggestion and capable of vivid hallucination. UFO abductees describe stereophonic sound effects before an abduction. This could be binaural beats transmitted via radio to a stimociever in each ear.

Electromagnetic Radiation (EMR), Extra Low Frequency (ELF) and ultrasonics were areas of research known to have been covered in the 60's by the US Defense Advanced Research Project Agency (DARPA) by Project PANDORA. Microwaves were examined with regard to possible use in mind control. The results indicated that pulsed microwaves can create leaks in the blood/brain barrier, induce heart seizures and create behavioral disorganization.

Further studies by the CIA-linked RAND corporation showed that insomnia, fatigue, irritability, memory loss and hallucinations could be caused by microwaves. The victim only has to be placed within an electromagnetic field to suffer the effects although internal electrodes amplify the wave. Microwaves can entrain the mind to Theta rhythms, in effect, a directed trance can be remotely induced.

In 1973, Dr Sharp of the Walter Reed Army Institute showed that pulsed microwaves could transmit spoken words directly into the brain. In 1974 J.F. Schapitz (funded by the Department of Defense) proposed to study the effects of radio frequencies in conjunction with hypnosis, "the spoken word of the hypnotist may be conveyed by electromagnetic energy directly into the subconscious parts of the human brain."

106

EVIL AGENDA OF THE SECRET GOVERNMENT

The subjects would be planted with a subconscious suggestion which could be triggered by cue word or image (ie. Jack Ruby, Sirhan Sirhan, Mark Chapman). Microwaves could provide an explanation for telepathic communication and repeat abductees. The implanted victim is targeted within a directed beam while their partner sleeps soundly beside them.

TOURETTE'S SYNDROME OF THE GODS

Secret messages could be sent directly into a unsuspecting persons brain using something as simple as music, television shows or movies. The magazine, *Excluded Middle* (issue seven, 1997), ran an article by Paul Rydeen called "The Song Remains the Same." In that article, Rydeen relates an experience when he was listening to the Eurythmics song "Sweet Dreams" playing on his car radio. "I realized the words were not anything like I remembered them. The music had become very thick and layered, and the words had changed to short looped phrases. In full multi-track style, the chorus played in the background while Annie Lenox sang 'Fuck me' over and over on one track, and 'Kill me' on the other. Lyrics that were not normally part of the song."

After listening to a tape of the song, Rydeen could not repeat the experience. Later, he heard on a radio broadcast of Frank Sinatra singing "That's Life," Sinatra saying something to the effect that if you don't like his lifestyle, he'll have his mob buddies come and "shoot your ass and you'll die." When Rydeen commented on these extra lyrics to his wife who was also listening, she denied hearing anything like what Rydeen had heard.

Paul Rydeen referred to his experiences as "Tourette's Syndrome of the Gods." Actually Rydeen might have experienced secret messages beamed directly into his and others minds, people sensitive enough to catch the message. Possibly these messages are meant for the subconscious mind, but for some reason Rydeen perceived the message consciously. The secret commands are probably broadcast on a carrier wave sent by unknown agencies, but not the performers of the songs. Music is simply a good way to open ones mind to hidden commands.

HIDDEN MESSAGES

There exists a very real possibility that the recent incidents of people suddenly "freaking out" and using guns to kill their families, co-workers or strangers, might be caused by mind control messages being sent out through the popular media. The reason though, continues to elude us.

Electronic mind control research is still being carried out under the guise of "Non-Lethal Weaponry." The purpose of this research is apparently the creation of programmed agents able to accomplish their tasks with no recollection of their deeds. US service men are now coming forward with claims that while on routine training courses they were drugged, hypnotized, placed under "electronic control" and subjected to extreme pain/pleasure mental conditioning.

A United States naval officer, during a lecture in the 70's, hinted that there might be some substance to their claims. He stated that recruits at the NATO HQ in Naples, Florida were strapped into their chairs to watch films of industrial accidents and African circumcision ceremonies in order to turn them into bloodcrazed killers who were then sent on assassination missions. The spirit of the Third Reich lives on.

The idea that the Third Reich, and possibly Hitler himself, might have survived the war and gone underground to continue their plans for world dominance, has a certain appeal to conspiratists and right-wing extremists in North America and Europe. Secret Nazi flying saucers have also gained a large following over the years as an alternative to the theory that UFOs are strictly from extraterrestrial sources.

EVIL AGENDA OF THE SECRET GOVERNMENT

Albert Speer, Germany's wartime armaments production minister and Reich Architect confidant to Hitler, felt that this was an important enough issue to state in the final volume of his post-war memoirs, *Infiltration*, 1981, in regards to an apparently unknown secret weapons plant located in an underground mine with 3,500 workers, the "the Fuhrer protocols make no mention whatsoever of this new weapon. It was not the 'flying saucers' which extreme right-wing circles now claim were secretly produced by the SS toward the end of the war and concealed from me. Our technology was quite remote from such flying objects."

More than fifty years after Hitler disappeared, the Third Reich is still a subject of controversy. There is no doubt that the Nazi dream continues today. According to a 1979 West German interior ministry report on terrorism, there were 24 Nazi groups in the country plus 52 more extreme right-wing organizations supporting many of the same principles. Some of these groups claim that they have direct contact with surviving members of the original Third Reich. Has the Third Reich survived, securing itself away from the prying eyes of the world? Hiding either in some remote location, or worse, living among us secretly planning for the day when they can rule again?

In 1980, a convicted bank robber in France claimed that some of the money from a $10 million Nice bank robbery was channeled to SS officers hiding all over the world. The robber said the money was being used to finance a new attempt to take over the world by Nazi terrorist rings. In Madrid, members of the Jewish community received death threats periodically from a terrorist organization calling itself "The Adolf Hitler 6th Commando of the New World Order."

Albert Speer states that Himmler and Hitler had plans for the SS to lock up 14 million prisoners after Germany won the war. Speer was given construction plans for barracks and camps large enough to hold this many men. The plan was for Himmler to become a great entrepreneur in postwar Germany, using the 14 million prisoners as slave laborers to rebuild the country and establish the new Germany as the strongest, most productive nation in the New World Order. Under the supervision of the Nazis, the world would have had no freedoms and would have faced the same brutality as did citizens of much of Europe during the war. Perhaps this dream of world domination has never really died, but instead, lay in wait for the perfect time to strike again.

The aftermath of the Third Reich still has a devastating effect on the world today, and will for generations to come. The citizens of planet Earth must remain constantly vigilant to the secret plans of the Nazis and their emulators. The consequences of allowing such groups to once again gain a stranglehold on the population is simply too horrible to contemplate.

From The Conspiracy Fringe

BORDERLINE STUFF

CHUPACABRAS! AND OTHER MYSTERIES by Scott Corrales.
The Chupacabra or "goat sucker" has struck in the heart of the Caribbean as it terrifies residents of Puerto Rico and ravishes live stock. Is it a poltergeist, a demon, or "something" created in the dark labs of the New World Order? **$21.95. Code: 3COM.**

VISITORS FROM TIME by Marc Davenport
Here are dozens of examples proving that UFOs use a technology so advanced they can literally warp space and time. Could they be from our own future, coming back to haunt us? **$17.95. Code: 3VFT.**

LOST WAS THE KEY by Leah Haley
A true account of the author's kidnapping, interrogation and even torture by uniformed men wanting information about her abductions. **$17.95 Code: 3LWK.**

JIMI HENDRIX: STAR CHILD by Curtis Knight
Was one of the greatest icons of the 60s under the influence of government inspired mind control, UFOs and spirituality oddity—or was he much more than just sex, drugs and rock and roll? A former close associate and band member gives the inner digs. **$15.00. Code: BJH.**

OTHER VOICES by George Hunt Williamson (and others)
Someone or "something" is screwing around with our broadcast frequencies. Even the late Sen. Barry Goldwater and various astronauts have reportedly received strange signals and messages from the unknown over ham radios, NASA broadcast bands, etc. **$15.00. Code: BOV.**

TESLA: MAN OF MYSTERY by Michael X.
Weird inventions of the strangest man who ever lived. Free energy, telephone calls to other planets, aura reading device. Weirdness supreme! **$10.00. Code: BTMOM.**

YOUR PASSPORT TO HEAVEN by Tim Beckley & Diane Tessman
Did the Heaven's Gate tragedy have to happen? Can we go to heaven onboard a UFO? Can the dead pick up the phone and call the living How close is Heaven to Earth anyway? **$15.00. Code: BPTH.**

OTHER WORLDS OTHER LIVES—DISCOVER YOUR TRUE COSMIC ORIGINS by Brad Steiger
Don't believe you were reincarnated from another planet into an earthly body? Is there some sort of "great experiment" and how might you fit in? **$15.00. Code: BOWOL.**

ANGELS & ALIENS
A non religious look at "articles of faith" in our lives that offers evidence that some friendly (but not "winged") beings keep us in their site to protect and obey. 14 articles in magazine format. **$7.95. Code: BAA.**

UNDERGROUND ALIEN BASES by Commander X
Aliens have established bases around the planet. An ancient tunnel system has existed on Earth since the time of Atlantis. Entrance ways can be found in many major cities. Some government and military officials have taken the side of the aliens. Here are bizarre stories about underground bases at Dulce, New Mexico; Groom Lake, Nevada; South and North Pole; Mt. Shasta, California, as well as in the Andes. Here are the first-hand reports of individuals who have been abducted, and have survived genetic experiments in these locations. **$15.00. Code BUAB.**

NIKOLA-TESLA—FREE ENERGY AND THE WHITE DOVE edited by Commander X
Here are Top Secret revelations concerning a newly-developed antigravity aircraft currently being tested inside Nevada's remote Area 51, as disclosed by a former military intelligence operative. This aircraft, which can fly three times higher and faster than any officially recognized plane or rocket, is based upon an invention of Nikola Tesla, one of the greatest "free thinkers" of all times, who arrived upon our cosmic shores in order to shape our technical and spiritual destiny. Tesla, the author reveals, came from another place to alert the world of impending danger (World Wars I and II), while at the same time offering "helpful solutions" to our problems and alternatives by which to greatly enhance our lives. In addition to previously unpublished material on Tesla's Other-Worldly "roots," here also are full details of the ongoing work of such modern-day inventors as Otis T. Carr,

EASY TARGETS
2 Who Were Silenced!

THE OCTOPUS: SECRET GOVERNMENT AND THE DEATH OF DANNY CASOLARO by Kenn Thomas & Jim Keith

In the blood-filled bathtub was the nude body of a blond man. The dead man had a dozen deep gashes in his wrists. When paramedics lifted the body they found a single-edged razor. On the desk sat an empty notebook, a legal pad with pages removed. THE OCTOPUS was Casolaro's name for an intelligence cabal he had documented involving a super-surveillance software misappropriated from a company by Ed Meese's Justice Department and sold illegally to police agencies world wide. Casolaro's research looked at bizarre murders among the Cabazon Indians involving tribal land; the privatization of CIA dirty tricks through a notorious security firm; Area 51, home of spy planes and rumored UFOs; Vietnam MIAs; and a strange human genome project, as well as the Illuminati secret societies of the 18th century. Hardbound, 180 pgs, **$22.00.** Order by title or code: **BODC.**

THE BENNEWITZ PAPERS
Engineer Paul Bennewitz obtained some remarkable film footage of mysterious craft hovering near the nuclear storage area of a New Mexico military base and  became sucked into a world of cover-ups and mind control. Shortly before he was silenced, he began receiving actual horrifying messages—and pictures over his TV set from supposed aliens. This is an amazing story of how one individual was driven to the brink due to the involvement of a "shadow branch" of the U.S. military. Cases of animal mutilations, secret bases are included in this privately published report NOT available in bookstores. Order by title or code: **BBZ. $25.00.**

Arthur H. Matthews and Howard Menger, who have perfected alternative methods of propulsion. $15.00. Code: BUTFE.

THE CONTROLLERS edited by Commander X

We are the property of an alien Intelligence! "Our" planet is a cosmic laboratory and we are but guinea pigs to those who have kept us prisoners on Earth. Humankind continues to face an all-out battle with those who have kept us as their slaves for centuries. Down through history, they have been known by different names: The Soulless Ones, The Elders, The, Dero, The Grays, The Illuminati and The Counterfeit Race. Yet, very few know the real identity and purpose of The Controllers, a strange, parallel race that is metaphysically programmed to do evil and, according to authorities, has complete control of our education process, major philanthropic foundations, the banking system, the media, as well as dominant influence over all worldly governments. $19.95 Code: BTC.

WELCOME TO UFO CENTRAL: PARANOIA FROM SPACE

STRANGE ENCOUNTERS: BIZARRE & EERIE CONTACT WITH UFO OCCUPANTS by Tim Beckley

Ten stories from the "twilight zone" of UFO weirdness. Terror onboard the mothership; UFO bases in Calif. etc. $15.00. Code: BSE.

PROJECT WORLD EVACUATION channeled by the Ashtar Command

EZ "good guys" says they're here to save our collective asses in cases of global conflict. You be the judge! $15.00. Code: BWE.

ROSWELL UFO CRASH UPDATE by Kevin Randle

Exposes the military coverup of the century and shows that ETs have really come to earth. $15.00. Code: BRUU.

EXTRATERRESTRIAL PAPERS by X

A UFO undergoes a close encounter and then starts receiving a series of letters in the mail from an entity who says he was onboard the craft at the time of the sighting and reveals amazing revelations regarding Earth's future. $12.95. Code: BETP.

UFO CRASH SECRETS AT WRIGHT PATTERSON AIR FORCE BASE by James W. Moseley

The story of a woman working in a photo lab at the base who sees pictures of a crashed UFO surrounded by a blockade of soldiers and dead aliens. Also recounts story of a space being who arrives at a large newspaper and leaves indentations in piece of metal with just his "fingertips." $15.00. Code: BUFOCS.

UFO DANGER ZONE: TERROR & DEATH IN BRAZIL by Bob Pratt

A personal study of 200 cases lead the author to believe that something frightening is taking place,

including murder and human mutilation by aliens or secret governments? $18.95. Code: BUDZ.

WHITE SANDS INCIDENT by Dr. Daniel Fry

Former scientists from White Sands Proving Grounds describes his trip onboard a UFO to N.Y. City and back in 15 minutes. $15.00. Code: BWSI.

LOST WORLDS, DNA & CLONING

STAR GODS: CLONE MASTERS OF THE UNIVERSE by Brad Steiger

At the dawn of antiquity did at least one group of ETs deliberately alter our DNA for their own purposes of manipulation of the human race? Has there been a "domestication" of humanity that has

trapped us on this planet? $15.00. Code: BS-GCM.

OVERLORDS OF ATLANTIS & THE GREAT PYRAMID by Brad Steiger

Here is archeological proof from multiple sources that the Great Pyramid was constructed with the assistance of the High Priests of Atlantis. Were these masters able to levitate the huge blocks of stone into place? What is inside the secret chambers? Will the Lost Continent rise soon? $15.00. Code: BOAGP.

UNSEEN KINGDOMS by Bill Cox

Are we surrounded by unseen entities who control aspects of our existence—for good and evil? Do angels, fairies, elementals, ETs and even Bigfoot "work together" toward some united cause? Comes with pyramid kit you can do experiments with. $15.00. Code: BUK.

FIRST TIME DISCLOSURES...AMAZING FACTS AS REVEALED BY CIA INSIDER

WHAT ARE THE PECULIAR CIRCUMSTANCES WHICH WOULD ALLOW THIS DEDICATED GOVERNMENT OFFICIAL TO REACH THE FOLLOWING CONCLUSIONS?

▲ Aliens known as "Skymen" have been coming to Earth's surface, and exploiting it for numerous years.

▲ Some of them have homes in caverns on the moon, Mars and its satellite Phoebus, Jupiter, as well as the Asteroids.

▲ Many more originate much nearer to the Earth's surface, from "Skyislands," or even from within the hollow of our planet, and possibly underwater hangers!

▲ That skychemicals and electrostatic gravity-like force of the alien Skyislands and skycraft have caused legions of accidents.

▲ Skymen have kidnapped a multitude of people and have long extracted blood from animals and men, as well as committed mysterious murders!

▲ Analysis of evidence that shows some spacecraft are gas-ejecting and that others utilize lines of magnetic force in their operation.

▲ Space Island effects on humans, including: odd fires; changes in climate; disastrous smogs; the straight line bands of global disasters; poisons from space; vortices of death from the sky, including the world wide haze of 1950.

THE SECRET UFO DIARY OF CIA OPERATIVE COMM. ALVIN E. MOORE
EXPOSING THE EXISTENCE OF THE ALIEN SKYMEN

Introduction by Commander X

As part of his extensive contribution to his country, Moore specialized in aeronautical engineering, was patent engineer and attorney for the Warner von Braun team of space scientists. He also served as a US. Patent Office Examiner specializing in aeronautics and propulsion; an assistant nautical scientist with the Navy Oceanographic Office; a CM intelligence officer and an American l/ice Consul. He had granted more than 50 US. patents on his own inventions mostly on aircraft, marine craft and automobiles. He also authored numerous technical and historical articles and books. $16.95—Code BSU